Poems for Pickin'

Poems for Pickin'

by Craig Pugh

Published May 2022 by The Writing Dog LLC
ISBN 978-0-9701140-3-7
Printed and distributed by
IngramSpark and Lightning Source

Cover design by Craig Pugh
Cover painting by Kate Loz

Other books by Craig Pugh:
A Pocketful of Poems
Ganja Tales

www.TheWritingDog.com

Dedication

For Audrey and Wayne
with love always

As I was throwing these poems into a volume, I found Kate Loz in Kyiv on
the internet and she painted the lovely front and back cover to this
book. Then Russia invaded and Kate disappeared.

I am proud, then, that the spirit of Ukraine encases this book through
Kate's artwork. And it is my fervent wish that one day she will be back in
Ukraine picking apples in an orchard with her family, just as she painted
on the cover.

*"Light breaks upon the horizon.
Here comes the dawn.
You are the poet.
Go sing your song."*

Al-Murzim
"The Herald"

Table of Contents

Johnny Appleseed And Me

They say Johnny Appleseed wore a tin hat
dressed in a coffee sack, walked barefoot
and loved animals so much he wouldn't
eat them. Me too, for I'm a vegetarian.

And I'm poor like Johnny was. Also like him
I eschew the fancy stuff as long as I can do
the thing I love, which is writing poetry.
For Johnny, that was growing apple trees.

Johnny was born in Massachusetts but
walked through Pennsylvania, Indiana
Ohio, Illinois and all down the Mississippi
River valley planting and selling apples
wherever he went. I can appreciate that.

I was born in Colorado but walk around
Omaha year after year with poems from
10th Street to 16th Street my west and east.
Then north and south bordered by Vinton
Harney and Leavenworth, all connected by
the railroad bridge I walk on back and forth.

To my dentist, my doctor, optometrist and
chiropractor; the coffee shop, grocery store
or bar. No matter whether I go, near or far
it's expected that I show up with a poem.

Johnny was a good spirit who saw beauty in
a valley full of trees. I'm like that with poetry.
I am a trifle jealous, though, that Johnny's got
the edge on me. You see, no matter how earnest

I try to be, most folks pick apples over poetry.
Just about everyone likes an apple. And if not,
hard cider can be made. That's tough to compete
with. I must admit: as a poet, I'm quite dismayed.

Poetry Pickin' Time

It's poetry pickin' time along the Platte.
The poems have grown fat upon the boughs.
They're ready to be picked now. Come bring
your bushel baskets! These poems are yours
for the asking. Sing with us and celebrate

the turning of the season and all the things
that give life reason. We've got cakes and
ciders and casseroles and jams and tarts and
apple pies with cinnamon hot from the oven.

Bring your heart and spirit, too, because
we've got lots of poetry for your soul. Join us
round the apple press. Let the stress fall off
your shoulders. Take a seat upon a bale
of hay. Stay awhile and help us revel in
the handsome crop of poems this year.

See the band about to play? There's Jim, tenor
in church choir, picking up his violin. Next to
him, Reverend Tim softly sings Amazing Grace.

Cupid flutters in with a playful grin, a quiver
full of arrows and a taut-laced bow. Notching
one, he lets it go at Hank and Sue pitching woo
over by the punch bowl where Ruth Anne bats
her eyes at Joe and slowly reaches for his hand.

Then – and what do you know? -- Grandma
even laughs at one of Grandpa's corny jokes.
Poetry's got them all in such a merry mood.

Young Will grabs his guitar and Mary her
violin and they join Jim and Tim playing
Sweet Clementine and Turkey in the Straw.

This causes Ma and Pa to get out on the floor
with son and daughter in the middle, all of 'em
kicking up their heels with lots of do-si-dos
and Virginia reels. Over in a far corner, women
talk and stitch a wedding quilt for Jennie Lynn.
She's to be a bonnie bride this spring. Behind
them a mother holds her newborn to a breast.

Out in the back yard the old dog gnaws on a bone
and scratches while in the barn the cats go crazy
after rats in the rafters and behind the bales of hay
Clara Bell and Bill play hide 'n' seek and patty-cake.

Young bucks have snuck out to take slugs from
a jug of corn liquor, then shout into the wind, flap
their arms up and down and walk around clucking
like chickens. Some drunken ones even stand on
their tiptoes and crow *Cock-a-doodle-doo!* while
others have turned wolfen and howl at the moon.

Two love birds sit by the pond gazing at heaven.
She says*: Would you look at that? It's Aldebaran.*
He replies: *No it's not you silly goose. It's Mars.*
She feigns anger and gently punches his arm.
This causes old mother duck to quack at them
for disturbing her rest by looking at the stars.

Down along the riverbank, the U.P. locomotive
chugging for Scottsbluff lets out a throaty blast
throwing cinders into the night and -- sure enough
behind the barn Jack kissed Lacy Mae on the lips
to which she said: Oh *Jack. That's quite the stuff!*

Yes, it's poetry pickin' time along the Platte.
From Omaha to Ogallala -- all across Nebraska
they've burst on the boughs to fill up the baskets
and celebrate the season, to keep the flame of life
burning bright in poetry pickin' time along the Platte.

Aurelia, What Color Is Your Hair Today?

I don't really need an avocado but I still think
I'll drive down to the Mercado just to satisfy
my curiosity because I absolutely have to see:
Aurelia, what color is your hair today?

Last week a happy streak of pink ran down
to your cheek. Rather *chic,* I thought. Then
yesterday your hair displayed all the rainbow
rays and even some colors in between. I swear.
Aurelia, sometimes you look seventeen!

Such colors you array. And that reminds me I
need to get some beans. Now I'm wondering:
maybe today your hair is green? If beans are bad
my backup plan will take me over to Jell-O, where
I'm sure I'll pause a minute and wonder if perhaps
last night you went and dyed your hair yellow?

And you know what? I'm hungry for pancakes so
I need maple *surple*. Which makes me ponder
if perhaps your hair isn't purple. Maybe I'll be over
by paper plates when I begin to contemplate the
tints and shades you may have dyed your hair today.

Or perhaps I'll be in liquor looking at a flask or over in
cosmetics perusing facial masks when the only question
I want to ask is: Aurelia, what color is your hair today?

And for sure I won't know what to say or do if I
show up and you've dyed it blue! *Ole*! I guess. I also
need a stopper for my sink, which makes me think
if once again you've gone and dyed your hair pink.

I love those colors how they show the flair in you
and say this girl's still got a kick or two. Indeed,
those rainbow hues are smiles to me expressing
the way you seize your day. You know, I'm jealous.
Why's that? Because my hair's turned gray!

You make me laugh and really get my sense of humor.
I'm grateful for that, which is why I'll walk up and down
the aisle at Mercado with a basket full of avocadoes
I don't need just so I can throw you a smile and say:
Buenos dias, Aurelia. What color is your hair today?

For Charles At Café Z

Thank God you set up shop a few years ago.
Before that I was in the throes of a Greek tragedy
what with walking up and down Sixteenth Street
wearing sackcloth and ashes, crying: "Woe is me!

Woe is me! I am without good coffee." You see, I was
out of my mind, so for special effects I'd lash my back
like an Arab penitent suffering under Allah's stern
punishment for not having good coffee. Seriously,
it was so bad all my gaskets were about to blow.

So thanks for opening Café Z and roasting all those
delicious coffee beans for those of us who can't forgo
the jolts of caffeine in that delightful brew. Thank you,

thank you very much, as Elvis would say. It's always
such a pleasure to take a small measure out of a hectic
day and pop in your shop to say: *Buenos Dias*, *Senor
Keenan*, which is about all the Spanish I can manage.

You are a hale fellow well-met who's led quite a life.
You're international. That's rare. You bring an ambience
and savoir faire to Omaha that make Café Z incomparable.

You're also large and lumber around like an elephant but
you're not a clumsy beast; you're actually sort of graceful
on your feet for a guy your size and possess a certain sense
of eloquence found only in the most intelligent elephants.

You've got the same huge wooden chairs from your old café
in Lima, Peru, and a great roaster that cracks aromatic coffee
beans. Then there's your office: which is actually a round table
with a top that spins yummy things around like ox-tail soup,
spicy roasted almonds, Caribbean rum and Kentucky bourbon.

This all amounts to an atmosphere that's hard to beat.
I remember a time or two when a good dozen people
gathered around and before the evening was through
we were all friends. Charles, that was because of you.

Add to that the fact that you're also generous to a fault.
Thank you Charles. I like that, especially when I'm involved.

What's more, you tell great stories: cars flying off
mountain roads high in the Andes, you getting shot down
in Vietnam. Before that you choppered through Angkor Wat,
you and the pilot eyeball-to-eyeball with the ancient carvings.

A SCUD missile once dropped in your backyard in Riyadh,
making the former Mrs. Keenan mad. She lost sight of
the notion that you were trying to make life epic and bold.

But the best tale you ever told was about your trip with
the Persian diplomatic delegation to Mongolia where you
almost had to eat rice-stuffed sheep's rectum, a thing
you said is their national delicacy. Yuck and what the heck!
I would definitely not be asking for seconds on sheep's rectum!

You're also one of the bravest men I've known. You proved
that in Vietnam many years ago when you stared death in
the eye getting blown out of the sky, just as you prove it now
by staring at him again today and saying: *That it? That all you got,
Big Guy?* So Charles, I'm glad we're friends and have spent some
idle hours together. It's been an honor and a pleasure to meet you.

Now, may I please have a pound of the Costa Rican?

She Knew I'd Come Back

Walking down the hill goes pretty fast.
I'm sober as a judge with a pocketful
of cash and my legs are good to go.

My feet are really flying down the walk.
I know Elvira waits for me with dirty talk
along with beers from twenty breweries
of which I can always find one to please.

My bar is just three blocks away. And what
makes it neat is I can play Pacman, pinball
Skee ball, shoot a rifle or drive racing cars.
Those are nice enough but Elvira's my game.

She's mistress of the dark and more than
a friend because she whispers sexily at me:
I knew you'd come back when I put a quarter
in. She's funny, fickle and such a teaser
it's hard to know which way to please her.

One moment she hollers: *Leave it alone!*
but then says *Put it in there!* with utmost
urgency. Elvira -- she's so encouraging.
First I lose and then I start to win. She gets
excited and starts screaming: *Yes! Oh yes!*
and I lose my head and shove more money in.

Ash grins at the bar. He keeps all the games
working right and knows he'll see me again.
Plus Andy's always good to pour me a beer
since he knows I like to keep one near.

Yes, walking down the hill sure goes fast. But my
legs that were good to go just mere hours ago
have a tendency not to last on the way back up.
It's a fact that long walk up really knocks me out.
Specially if I drank a few of those oatmeal stouts!

A Thirsty Poet Writes At A Bar

There's a million bars in this old town
running up and down the windy streets
but I go to one in particular where Ash
the bartender, enjoys reading poetry.

And some days when I'm feeling fair
I perch on my favorite barstool there
and Ash pours me a nice cold ale and
I settle in to write with paper and pen.

I've written poems before that really
choke Ash up. On such occasions when
he reads them, he nods approval and says:
Oh man. You really wrote a good one here.

Next thing I know a beer appears. I look up
and see a tear in Ash's eye and he replies:
This one's on me on account of that poem.

He's a good sport; I won't deny it. Yet for all
of that he's a stern wordsmith, too; you see
I've sat there before flipping him poems that
he reads and then shakes his head no, saying
that when I see him crying I'll know I wrote
another good poem, and until then: no beer.

So today's a little rough, for I'm down on my luck
and lack a buck to buy a beer. It's a sad fact indeed
that I'm riding a losing streak drinking water for free
at the bar, wondering where my creative juices are.
No -- my muse won't speak to me although I'm dry
as a stone and would love to soak my bones in beer.

So could you do me a favor and take this poem down
to Ash? And when you return, let me know if he's crying?
I'm parched, I tell you, and just dying for an ice-cold beer.

The White Cat

White Cat, the mark of death was on your head.
You carried such hurt on your face and more than
a few scars attesting to your fights to stay alive
down here on Sixteenth Street in between the
parking lots, dumpsters and back alley ways.

And yet you were so sweet. God bless you, little guy.
You never nipped or bit or threatened. You rubbed
against our feet and ate the treats we set out for you
at night. Slept on the beds we made for you inside
the courtyard and under the bushes on the sidewalk.

We saw you'd never been held or loved. Didn't know
what affection was. White Cat, all of us already had cats
otherwise any one of us would have taken you in.
Well, except for Aiyana and Brian. Against all advice
(*The cat could be diseased: best leave him alone*.)
they decided to adopt you. And you got in the crate
and let them take you to the Omaha Humane Society
for a free checkup. We only wanted the best for you.

The next day when they went to get you they heard
the awful words: *That cat is no longer in the facility.*
What!? Oh no! What do you mean? And Brian had to be
escorted from the facility. We're so sorry, little guy.
We had no idea they'd do you in. We console ourselves
that you must have had something incurable that was
going to get you in the end. So you didn't die of disease
like a wretch in the street. And before they put you down
you felt the love from all of us in the apartment courtyard.

We saw a fighter in you, a little boy-cat who got dealt
some bad cards and still hung on. We saw it took all
your strength just to stay alive. You poor little guy.
You never had a name or a home. You were worth
so much more. You were worth at least this poem.

Hound Dog's Chain Gang Of Love

Through these thin apartment walls I hear her
tear in to you each morning with her whiplash
voice boxing your ears. One verbal slap after
another, ending with: *I'll take my baby and leave!*

And you, brother, far as I can tell, put up with it.
You -- a thug-bumpin' ghetto-bustin' six-foot stack
of baggy-pants trouble, on your knees in front of
that woman with your tail tucked between your
legs like a submissive dog. It's not dignified.

Then I see you go out at the crack of dawn to work
on a road crew all day long, because yesterday I got
gas and saw you in a bright-green construction vest
shoveling hot asphalt off the back of a truck. It was
ninety-two and your clothes were sweated through.

On your days off I see that you are loving, kind and
never raise your voice playing with the little girl.
I watch you out the window drawing chalk pictures
of hearts on the sidewalk with her. You'd think love
like that would be worth something. But not to
your woman. No sir. She keeps your leash tight.

I see your hound dog look and think of the price
you must pay to be shackled to the chain gang
of her love. And why on Earth you pay the toll
even though it makes you less than whole.

Senior Center Poetry Class

(for Wildy)

Jambo! Jean. And what's new, Stew? Susan
good to see you as always. We're poetry geeks
who meet once a week at the Intercultural
Senior Center on Center Street, seeking a
verse or two in order to make sense of things.

You could say we get centered in The Center.
We put our troubles aside to spend an hour
inside a circle of light in a well-lit room
where we take delights in flights of poetry.

It's actually quite a treat, if nothing else
for all the people you meet. Jean has come
a long way from The Congo, Rwanda and
a refugee camp. She's a survivor, a woman
of great strength, grace and dignity. With her
I stumble around and try to speak Swahili.

I think Stew's a good ol' boy like me who tries
not to get too far ahead of his skis. I like that
and sure hope he knocks out that poem about
Nebraska football games he went to as a kid.
I'm glad I can be here to help him write it.

Susan's from New England and has a mind like
a steel trap. Just last week in class she recited
a poem about some frogs in the sand who got
run over by a dune buggy on Martha's Vineyard.
It was a funny poem and I wish you were there.

So for sure: The Senior Center's a place where
the four of us meet to twist up words in the air.

12

And even though four may not sound like much
to you, Emily Dickinson said it only takes a clover
and a bee to start a prairie -- and reverie. So now
you see how we four can grow our own poems.

I'm the reverie. Stew? I believe he's the clover
while Susan and Jean I think are the bees.

But I have to tell you something about those three
that's funny and ironic to the supreme. They think
I teach them, but they're the ones teaching me.

They're teaching me about faith and persistence
about hanging on and not giving up. And that's why
I go to the senior center each week to talk with Stew
and Sue and Jean to find a little art in life with poetry.

And as for starting a prairie I think we just began one
today because a man walked in and said: *Greetings.
I am Saddiq from Sudan.* And he took a seat with
a smile big and wide. See? Now we four are five.

I Saw It All

He walked into my poetry class at
the senior center -- frazzled, old and
grey, holding forth a fine leather bag.
I am Saddiq from Sudan, he said, *and
I make leather goods with my hands.*

That's beautiful, I replied. Thank you
for coming in the room. We're looking
at a poem about India today written
by a guy named Kipling. Sound good?

Saddiq nods assent and sits next to Jean
who is from the Congo and speaks French
and Swahili. I go over the rhyme and meter
in the poem. Saddiq speaks Arabic and
part of my job is to teach them English.

Jean survived the genocide in Rwanda
years ago as a girl although her father's
side of the family was "wiped out,"
as she says. Saddiq, I later learned,
has just escaped the slaughter in Sudan.

So I'm reading a line of Kipling, and Saddiq
took off his glasses and wiped his brow and
at that moment he seemed as old somehow
as Methuselah himself, weary with life and
all the sorrow it had brought his way.

In fact, Saddiq was all Saddiq had left in life.
He had himself and a leather bag. His wife,
his children, his land and farm -- all gone.

I saw it all when he wiped his brow. His life
became crystal clear somehow: I saw bones
in the sand, the rib cage of a child, babies

with swollen bellies. Drought and famine.
Plague and death followed by infestation.

Four Horsemen of the Apocalypse riding out
of the desert's hot breath, scimitars flashing.
People trembling before death and genocide.
Rape and terror. Dying cries of young girls.

Mothers with skull-faced newborns pressed
against shriveled breasts. Spirits cleft from
bodies. Vultures picking at dry-rag corpses.
And a shiver of fear rose in my chest.

But I pressed on, got class done and Saddiq
walked by on the way out and showed me
a piece of leather, his name stamped on it
and keys on one end. *You like?* He asked.

I saw the craftmanship in it and told him
how nice it was. His face lit up with a smile
then and he said: *I will make one for you*!

Oh that Saddiq! He strives to be of service.
To give something to someone in spite of all
that he's lost. And I realized this is how Saddiq
finds ways to keep going, and doesn't give up.

He's trying to love and to be loved. To do
something for somebody else. And it amazes
me how he gets past the blows he's received.

Because carrying all that pain can't be easy.
But I see light and spirit in his eyes. And it
shows me that he found ways to survive.

Saddiq is a definite rascal. And surely one of
a kind. With six simple words – *I will make one
for you* – he renewed my faith in mankind.

Helping My Son Move

We took the pictures down from the wall
next to the kitchen where we drank all that
alcohol and made so many meals. Such a deal.
And fun. In fall we watched football on TV.
Winter brought Jayhawk hoops and go KU!

Five years flew past. Man, that was fast. Now,
and at long last, you have a place of your own:
a yard and a garden -- not an apartment. A home.

We hauled plenty of our shared boxes up from
the basement, each one laden with memories of
years gone by, years spent trying to get somewhere.

Me the father, you the child. You and me, my son,
spinning through time together. And we remarked
on how funny it is that things once so important
no longer were. We spoke of bosses, good and bad;

the sergeant's stripes I once had when G.I. Joe
was your dad. Your sister's name came up and so,
too, a beloved dog that died. And by gosh! I saw
that letter of recommendation I once got

from a four-star general. How proud I was then,
your mother too, although you were too young
to remember. Anyway, those days are long gone now
and those artifacts, cards and pictures that once meant
so much sit in the trash. That was a sober reckoning.

Change, we mused, making trips back and forth
to the dumpster to throw away our pasts, *is good.*
Elsewise we're better off dead because we'd be boring
and hating ourselves for it. *Crisis – it makes us act and
that's a good thing.* Yes sir. That's exactly what we said.

All of that may be true and without a doubt I'm happy
for you; yet still I went to sweep your place last night
and it hit me so hard how empty of spirit it was inside
without you. Son, I damn-near got down and cried.

To My Mean-Girl Neighbors

One day you will know what I know.
You will watch the years fly by and
evaporate before your eyes, each
bringing a new heartache or care.
Another loss, more grey hair.

You may have to dance with cancer
as I do and wonder if your life will
soon be through. Maybe you'll get
a brain tumor. What's handy then is
a sense of humor. You won't have time
for all your petty fights and fits of anger.

Your hearing or vision may go. You could
get a series of strokes that paralyze you
and put you on a walker or stroller.

There's diabetes, and let's not forget
heart attacks and high blood pressure
or all those pill bottles on your dresser
for all your eczema and fits of depression.

You could even cop liver cirrhosis, miss
some chances or get a wrong diagnosis.
Then oh my dears and if you please; I see
you are scheduled for colonoscopies and
get to work your way through your fifties.

Yes, it's time to get on with all of that.
Hot flashes, your gut, your GI tract and
rolls of fat. It's called aging. So really?

Feuding with neighbors who bring you corn
from the market and cake on a plate; people
who act decently toward you? In between
rounds of chemo, who's got time for all that?

Apparently you two do. Wow. What can I say?
Other than sorry you choose to live in such a
wretched way where you bypass love for hate.

Because one day you will know what I know
when your dreams march out of your heart.
When you get lost in the dark. When your lover
departs. When you can't find the loose ends
and tie them back together to make amends.

When you bury friends, parents or lose a child.
Then you will know how it feels to be wild with
grief. You won't have time for courtyard beefs.

You'll know what it feels like to be the victim.
To be falsely accused. Maybe then you'll stop
throwing stones and attacking your neighbors.

Being unkind to people who do you favors, then
turning around to complain they're against you.
Oh boo hoo! Trust me. We're not. Honestly,
we're too busy just trying to survive and get by
rather than spend our days worrying about you.

Old Friends, Brick Walls And Dead Ends

Old friends, I haven't seen you in years and no doubt
won't ever see you again. I wonder if you know how
often I think of all the great fun we had back then.

Time got away from us. Then jobs, transfers and
marriages occurred. Then a divorce. The future
blurred. One day I looked up; you were out of state.

Whatever plans we had – too late. Then politics
came between us, and a silly Facebook argument,
for Pete's sake. Left unspoken was the difference in
the money we made. You toasted with champagne
from Veracruz. Me? South Omaha, cheap booze.

Still, the years flew past way too fast. And I lost count
of the times I've thought of you and sighed. Somehow
we became ships far away; specks on mental horizons.

Sentimental? Perhaps. I plead guilty to looking at years
past and wondering how you and I grew so far apart, we
who used to shoot the shit, borrow wrenches, work on
each other's cars, drink beers and chase bawdy wenches.

Mark, you were "Murf the Turf" when we were G.I.s at
Fort Ben Harrison, good ol' Company B, First Battalion.
We drank in your barracks room, called it Turf's Tavern.

Jeff, when I knew you at KU we played foosball like crazy
fools. You were "Barrage Garage." I was "The Dixie Demon."
Would I go back for a night of that at the old Gaslight Inn
on Jayhawk Boulevard in Lawrence, Kansas? You bet!

Dennis, my brother, my best friend. You fell down a flight
of stairs at fifty and met your end. Your death is something
I've tried all these years to comprehend. You were truly an
angel looking for your wings. You just found them so early.

Ben, you married, moved to The Big Apple to find your dream.
Me? Still stuck in Nebraska with a broken one. Same old story.
I'd just like to know how in the heck does all this happen?

Steve, you moved to Colorado. I wish I could go. I like weed
as much as you do – very much so. I was also born in Greeley.
Why is it, then, when I look out my window I see Omaha?
It's not half as cool or touchy-feely as downtown Greeley.

Old friends, how I wish we hadn't drifted off into the slipstream.
I tried holding on to you but I was as busy as you were punching
a clock, mowing my yard, trying to get somewhere and trying to
remember what day of the week it was that trash got picked up.

So I regret that I must accept these brick walls and dead ends
for old friends I'll never see again. Guys, I just hope you found
me as good a friend as I found you. You're not here physically.

Yet in my memory you're very much alive to me, the same
good company you were so long ago when you and I were
younger and more carefree. Really? That was us? Guess so!

When I pause from life's demands my mind returns to us back
then and thoughts of being such good friends. Memories of you
are always kind and I'm grateful our friendship stood the test
of time. I carry thoughts of us in more ways than I can say.

Acupuncture

I'd never had acupuncture before. Have you?
So I didn't know what to expect, then, when
I went for my first visit. Soon I'm in a room
chillin with Sara, who's got a master's degree
in this stuff and tells me to relax and not worry.

I breathe a sigh of relief and tell her my story
about how I broke both bones in my right leg
just above the ankle. "Fine," she says. "Hop up
on the bed and take your shoes and socks off."

I'd seen some needles in rows in a box when
I came in the room. Looked like a bunch of them
packed up tight against one another in long rows.

I didn't give those darts much thought but when
Sara stuck the first one in it sure got my attention.
I almost shouted: "Holy Shit!" since (Sonofabitch!)
it pierced my flesh and so did the rest of them, with
poke and prick and stab and sting one after another.

I tried to go Zen but Sara kept sticking those damn
things in. Their little needle noses kept poking little
holsies in my skin as I went ouch! ouch! and ouch!
until a whole bunch of them stuck out the bottom
of my foot and down both sides of my right ankle.

She got my left foot, too, and just when I thought
we were through she put a move on my right hand
and stuck more needles behind my pinkie finger!
I said: *What's this? I'm looking at four or five of those
dad-gum little buggers stuck in my arm by my wrist!*

And she wasn't done yet. She stuck more pins in
my left ear, hit the lights and said: "See you in a bit."
I ask: "What's a bit?" She replies: "Thirty minutes."

Now, I was on a nice buzz when I walked into the place.
I'd been up early and was writing at a madman's pace
and wasn't quite ready to slow my stroll and call it quits.
And Sara said thirty minutes. Holy cow. What to do now?
Well, there's prayer. I began silently reciting a favorite.

*From the point of light within the mind of God, let light
stream forth into the minds of men. Let light descend
on Earth.* That worked for a minute, but I lost the trail
only picking it up again because I had lots of time to kill.

Sooo . . . *Let pain bring due reward of light and love. Let
my soul control my outer form and life and all events . . .*
and I fell asleep. When I woke I didn't know where I was
and in the startle of it and half-sitting up I brushed some
of the needles off my ear and got scared for some reason.

I felt like I'd messed up. So I lay back down real still and
tried getting mellow. After a while I saw myself floating
up by the ceiling, and I looked down at myself on the bed
and thought: *This is strange.* But I fell asleep again and only
woke when Sara burst in and started pulling out the pins.

Now you know why I couldn't get out of there too soon.
I said goodbye, auf wiedersehen, sayonara and adieu.
Don't call me; I'll call you. I drove home, got in bed and
went to sleep. Now I gotta decide about next week if I
want to go see Sara and let her stick me all over again.
You could say the decision's got me on pins and needles.

Call Me To Prayer

All along the coastal towns
King Neptune takes a drink.
Out at sea, boats sink. Lord,
for all the drowned sailors
help me say a prayer.

In the cities, on the streets
people can't make ends meet.
Cops show up and start to beat.
Mothers' voices cry out in pain
reminding me to once again
add my voice to yours.

Help me melt the hard-hearted.
Help me get the peace talks started and
feed your energy into the minds of man.
Help me serve others whenever I can.

For all the children on the border
who cry in cages for their parents.
For all the black men who can't breathe
when the police officer takes a knee.
Lord – please -- call me to prayer.

There's so much need for more goodwill
People go hungry but crops rot in fields.
I look around. So much is wrong.

Folks young and old always on phones.
Don't look up, it's a government drone.
Animals scared, but must go forward.
Man who kills them got the Covid.

Humankind fouled the very air. Virus blows
everywhere. I know if any of this will change
I have to sit down and call your name.
Lord, won't you call me to prayer?

I Rise In The Light

They took me to the guillotine
and tied me to the board, then
shoved me forward face-down
with my head upon the block.
And the bastards chopped it off.

But my spirit rose in the light.
It rose to live another life.

And once I lay in a miner's cave
my body crushed by tons of rock.
But my spirit rose between the cracks.
All of Earth couldn't hold it back.
I rose in the light to live another life.

I also sailed the bounding blue
as a sailing man on the Spanish Main.
Then one day a massive wave blew up
and took me down to a watery grave.

I was wet and I was drowned, but only
for a minute because my spirit healed
itself and shook off all the water in it.
Like a bubble, then, I rose in the light.

I awoke in an age Medieval where
a wicked priest so very evil tied me to
a burning pole so he said to save my soul.

In the flames and on my death I told him
to save his breath. Only God calls me home.
That's why I keep singing my warrior song.

I rise each morning, indomitable, indefatigable,
unbeatable -- Phoenix-like, steady and bright
with my heart on fire, hands outstretched
for the love of Christ, I rise in the light.

I'm Coming Through

I know I don't look like much to you
and you stuck me in your discount bin
to wallow in a dusty corner in the back
of your mind. I got it. I'm Five-and-Dime.

You marked me low and now I know
you think I'll never find a way to win.
Thus I labor in your give-a-way rack
with the broken toys that don't wind up.

The little monkey who can't beat his cup.
The poor pale moon who forgot her tune
and doesn't remember her lunar phases.
Odd books, lost little books missing pages.

Now all of these things may be true but
boy oh boy do I have some news for you.
I'm coming through. I wasn't born to love
or money and fortune wasn't mine to claim.

I never knew the right people nor learned to
play the game. Didn't schmooze or drink booze.
Didn't run in fancy tennis shoes or expensive
jogging suits. I don't care. I'm used to it.

I expect it will be raining and the boss will be
complaining. For the chips to be down. For the
odds to be slim. For the uphill slog always in
the cold and even if I don't get paid. So what?

I'm the guy who's going to win because no matter
how steep the grade I'm going to do what I always do.
I'll be coming through. Because that's what I do.

How Will We Know It's You?

Jesus, I know you said you'd be with us
until the end of ages and that one day
you would come back and save us. In fact,

I pray each year during the May full moon
when you appear over the Wesak Valley
in the Himalayas to bless mankind with
your loving grace and reassurance.

But I do have just one burning question.
How will we know it's you when you return?
First, won't they throw you in the looney bin
for saying you're Jesus Christ, the son of God?

Surely the bishops and cardinals and priests
would say that notion's too odd to contend with.
Remember two-thousand years ago when those
freaking Pharisees called your words blasphemy
put thorns on your head and nailed you to a cross?

Seriously, at the very least you'd need an attorney.
The headline will read: "Man locked up for saying
his father is God and we are all to be forgiven."
Imagine -- if someone wanted a visit from Jesus
they'd have to go to jail and post your bail!

If jail's eluded you'll need marketing agents with
lots of social media savvy to help you navigate
the airwaves and get your message to the masses.

Specials on HBO? Maybe Netflix. But oh the pressure
would be on for you to perform all your old tricks
like turning water to wine and making the blind see.
Feeding the multitude with a few fish. Raising Lazarus.

Then the Republicans will say: *What is this? Why,
the man's a socialist! Taking money from the rich
to give it to the poor? That's rubbish and nonsense!*

What's more, when guys saw you making out so well
being mellow they'd get jealous and imitate you just to
get girls and win friends. Everyone would claim to be you.
Then what a mess we'd be in. Want Jesus? Which one?

Now I hear this year engineers put speakers on poles
all over the Wesak* Valley, just like at a drive-in movie
so rich kids can sneak in the trunks of their parents' Jags
and Range Rovers streaming over the mountain for some
popcorn and bourbon-and-cokes from the soda fountain.

Lord, look what they've done in Your sacred and holy name.
I was hoping for something other than the same old game.
Not a bartender mixing craft cocktails from a top shelf while
a ragged old beggar sells amulets blessed by the goddess herself.

Not to mention all those old Deadheads stoned silly on hash
trekking up the trails as Learjets glide in one after another
to land on a runway built for the billionaires who are so vain
they'll think the full moon is about them. Oh Jesus Christ.
How do you get your message across in a mess like that?

I know it's one for the money and two for the show, but
Lord, when you come back, how will we know it's you?

* Some people believe Jesus reappears on Earth once a year above a Tibetan
valley to affirm his vow to mankind: *Lo, I am with you always, to the very end of
the age. Matthew 28:20*

I'm Going to Heal You From Omaha

(for Kelly)

You are one of the best people I know so there's no way
you got cancer and may have to go. I can't accept that as
a done deal. That's why I'm going to heal you from Omaha.

You heard me right and I already started because I hold you
up in prayer each morning at five and bath you in a halo
of soothing white light. Stretching my fingers and raising
my arms I send my cry of healing out into the universe

for you, pulling down great handfuls of cosmic energy and
pushing them your way in Portland. I wave my arms back
and forth like a fly-fisherman trying to make the perfect cast
on your cancer and bring you the rest and relief you deserve.

Then I get vigorous and picture myself as a Roman catapult
hurling huge fireballs of healing light that whoosh through
the air and strike home on your bad cells, blasting them to
kingdom come with the fury of Genghis Khan's horsemen.

I also attack your cancer like an axe-wielding Anglo-Saxon
chopping up hordes of invading Vikings. I fear not. I am clan
Robertson, and true to my Scottish word, fierce when roused.

Yet still I'm not done as all of the above is just Step 1 because
I also sit in lotus for determined meditation amping energy up
and down the chakras of my spine. Once my hands are full of
electricity I thrust them out and let it flow through me and
WHAM! hit you hard with universal healing and Reiki rays
that soothe your ills and help you recuperate. These jolts
of healing beams are near impossible for any cancer to take.

29

They're not a pinch, nor a smidgen; rather, they're a hundred
ka-jillion kilowatts of healing power searching up and down
your intestines for cancer cells to swat. You see, being Leo,
the sun's mine to harness. And the universe says I can if I think
I can. Do I think I can? Sure. Why not? I'm giving it a shot.

How so? Well, I'll have you know I recently drove to the zoo
and jumped in the pond with the seals so I could bark and flip
my fins for you. Shoot. That one made the evening news!

And today I planted myself deep in the ground with tulip bulbs
called *Love Comes 'Round.* So now this spring when I'm in bloom
I'll be the picture of health growing beautiful flowers for you.

And I've yet to mention my cedar broom that I sweep all day
through your cancer rooms and take the refuse to the front stoop
where the old hausfrau waits with her scouring brush to say *Raus!*
Get off my porch, you filthy shoes. Get off! Get off! Get off!

And it's amazing yet true that hot blue Sirius, steady in his burning
pauses in admiration at my radiant rays so ultra-bright that even he,
the hottest star, turns green with envy. Friend Sirius salutes me
with a wink and says *Good Day, Sir. And luck be with you on your*
journey! Then sends me extra healing rays of burning just for you.

If I put it another way I can say your cancer is Sodom and Gomorrah
and you can think of me as healing fire burning down your wicked cells
to the ground unrepentant sinning and degenerate dividing.

Walk away with me, Abraham, Lott and Edith. Neither will we
dare look back on your burning cancer city. *Veni, vidi, vici.*
My flames will do their work. You see, my voltage meter broke
a long time ago. First it blew one fuse, then two; that's when I said
what's the use in trying to regulate my unbridled healing power?

I burned in earnest then, roaring in on your sick cells, scorching them
with my prairie fire. When the fire gave out I turned to air and flew in
on a wing and a prayer with a host of angels singing a hallelujah chorus.

And then there's times I play it slow by bathing you in a warm
and loving glow. Think of a full moon at midnight on an Alpine
meadow covered in snow. Can you see the healing crystals
sparkling in the air? I watch you breathe them in for cellular repair.

I also picture you shopping in the produce aisle or in your kitchen
mixing a blender drink, then dashing out the door and jogging
to the gym so you can bust out some weights. Later I see you
sitting on a bench lacing up skates for the rink. Oh I know --
it's a busy schedule, but you've got a lot of healing to do.

Some laugh and say such long-distance healing can't be done.
But I've got a secret: my furnace is the sun. I'm no Icarus
poor fellow who got it all wrong with his waxen wings. No,
my healing rays are made of surer things like prayers, fireballs
and healing beams. And I've also got seals at the zoo, chakras,
the German hausfrau and tulip bulbs. What do you think?

See how I've thrown everything but the kitchen sink at you?
That's how I know we're going to get you fixed. It's baked
in the cake. I'm just one-hundred percent, razor-focused
absolutely positive-sure I'm going to heal you from Omaha.

It won't be easy, but that's okay. It's just a simple matter of
willpower, determination, perspiration and a little elbow grease.

As luck would have it, I possess these qualities in rich profusion and
I'm glad to use them on you because you've always been one of
the best people I know; so, I figure you got all this coming to you.

I'm Going To Shine So Bright This Year

I'm going to shine so bright this year I'm shooting for
the biggest stars of all like Sirius in the throat of the Big Dog,
Canus Major. At Number One he's so much brighter than
our own sun. That's hot but I'm not deterred to land on him.
Heck. I might even leap on over to Procyon in *Canis Minor.*

He's the Little Dog but still in the Top Ten for shining.
One dog's the major, the other the minor but both canines
suit that wish of mine to be a brighter shiner this year. True
I may get scorched but I refuse to stay on the porch since
I'm going to run with the big dogs in the stars this year.

It's all because I spent the winter in the garage building
a flying machine that sorta looks like a car but sprouts wings
and travels to the stars. It's pretty neat. I get those wings in
and out with pedals down by my feet. Sure, my space craft
rattles and shakes, but I do too. So as for getting me into space

I reckon it will do. I powered my little buggy with a VW Beetle
engine block I got on sale from U-Pull-It Junk Lot. The motor spins
two turbines (blades, actually, that I pulled off lawnmowers from
Sol's Pawn Shop). See? Told ya I'm a sure-shot. I even strapped
a backup battery pack to it from my weed-eater in the backyard
so I'm double-dog guaranteed to zoom up there with the stars.

You can see NASA's got nothing on me and I don't need no Ph.D.
Jeez-Louise. I figure stuff out all by myself and I already thought of
everything else. That's why I wrapped my spacecraft in aluminum foil
(so my blood doesn't boil) and also grabbed my motorcycle windshield
to hold in front of me on my journey through Saturn's rocky rings.

So I'm serious about Sirius. However, if I miss him there's plenty's left
in the Top Ten, like Canopus at Number Two. He's for smooth sailing
that's for sure, anchoring as he does the floor of a celestial ship
once sailed by Jason and the Argonauts in Greek lore. I know it's far.

But I've got my sights set on reaching the brightest stars like Arcturus
at Number Three glowing in the crotch of Bootes, the Bear Herder.
I don't know why Arcturus is down there but I don't think Bootes
will rip a fart and foul the air. I'm pretty sure he will keep it clear.

So Sirius, Canopus and Arcturus – Numbers One, Two and Three.
After that there's Vega, Capella and Alpha Centauri at Four, Five
and Six; then blue super-giant Rigel shining bright on Orion's thigh.

And you know what? If my astral dash ends up in a space-splash
I've programmed my craft to land on Achernar in the River of Stars.
At Number Ten he's hot and white and fusing boatloads of hydrogen.
That rascal comes in at more than seven times the size of our sun
and if I reached him I would tell myself: Hey Craig, well-done!

Then I would know what to do. I would shine each day in 2022.

Stellarum Nocte

I looked up at the sky tonight and
craziest thing I ever saw. Leo,
rising, raised his paw and roared
scattering a slew of stars across
the universe wheeling overhead.

Pisces with her school of fish swam by.
Virgo slid past, swinging her scythe
and Gemini flew in and out the jewels
of Orion's belt searching for his twin.

Mercury spun madly on his top dashing in
the thick and thin of Neptune's foggy weather
before suddenly disappearing altogether.

Even Venus lost her bearing and went sailing
off into the rings of Saturn, getting stuck
amongst the rocks in the orbit pattern.

Jupiter Rex, laboring under the strangest hex
kept taking running leaps and trying to spin
but couldn't find the right gear to put it in.

Meanwhile, the Big Dipper -- he's such a sneaker
but I'm a peeker and I spied him filling his cup up
to the brim with giant scoops of comet ice-cream.

Then over on the side of the page I saw Aquarius
ushering in her age pouring streams of knowledge
from her urn into Eridanus, the river of stars
upon which Achernar the Viking Ship sailed past
with Vela, Carina and Volans pulling at the oars.
Up front with his hammer? You guessed it: Thor.

Crab scampered across to stab the sea goat
on his heel while Scorpio saw the advantage
and raced in for the kill, the noise of which
woke Mars from a nap and got him so mad
he attacked an innocently passing asteroid.

This made the king of beasts roar again, saying
That's enough of that! And with a lash of his
blue-white tail, Leo knocked Mars into jail and
ordered all the stars and planets back in
the paths of their proper heavenly trails.

Moon rose then, blushing and full of grace.
I gazed in awe at the splendor of all I saw,
then walked back inside and went to bed.

Fire, Earth, Wind. Then Drowning.

A huge star burned so gloriously bright and true
but I looked at it and laughed because it paled
in front of my love for you. That's right:

My love for you was bigger than a star.

In fact, I snuffed that star out like a candle,
handed it back to itself and said: *Sunny Jim.*
If you got a Daddy, I'd be running home to him.

Then came a wind of great force and proportion –
cosmic, galactic. Landscape distorting. Trees, buildings
. . . all down. I shrugged and said: *That all you got?*

Because that wind was so much less than the breath
I held in my lungs for you; in fact, a minute ago
I sneezed and wiped out Timbuktu, a trifling matter
easily disposed with a single blow from my nose.

Trinidad's next, I suppose. Followed by Barbados.

Then Mother Earth lost her mirth and cracked herself
with an earthquake, fooling everyone but me; you see,
I knew she only quaked to equal my heartbreak over you.

Rain fell to match my tears when Mother Earth broke.
But it wasn't the type of rain one can reasonably explain
because it fell for hundreds of days in hundreds of ways

jumping levies, bursting dams; smashing floodgates,
smothering prime land. Noah drifted by in his ark and
what the heck – kangaroos jumped up and down
on the deck while all the dogs barked Arf! Arf!

I snickered. Not to bicker with rain, but I explained that
I've cried more tears than that over you over the years.

I just have. Tears that drove me to a lonely shore
where I stood in the boiling surf to implore:
Why God, must the one I love hate me so?

Just then Neptune broke water out at sea, rising
in dripping majesty taller than the tallest building,
roaring louder than Niagara Falls and ripping at
dangling seaweed tangled in his dready beard.

And sure, I let out a cry of surprise when I spied
a great white shark impaled and flipping its tail
on a prong of Neptune's trident, which he thrust
high over his head. Then? Bated breath, my friend!

And here came the wind again – waves, too
as Neptune let out a horrible hullabaloo, saying:
Who do you think you're looking at, Pinhead?

I said: *Uh, Neptune? God of the Sea?* but that old man
just stared at me and sent a tsunami my way. I turned
to run but could not, rooted as I was to the spot while
he shouted: *Here's a message from the one you love*!

Then all the pain you inflicted on me sucked me into
the boiling sea and swirled me down, down, down and
drowning into the cold dead bottom of your black heart.

You Can't Leave. You're Part Of Me.

You don't see the hairs depart my head.
Where else would they grow instead?
And you don't see my nose fall off my face.
That's because it knows its place on me.

Nor do my lips drop off my chin since
they'd just have to get back up there again
or my eyes pop out of my brow and slip
into my pockets since they know somehow
I'll only stuff them back in their sockets.

And my fingers don't rip off my hands and
say adios no more than my toes depart
my feet and walk away without the rest me.

Same goes for my legs that don't break off
beneath my knees and take off on their own
because they both know they belong to me.

In fact, my brain and mouth and eyes that see
are all the many parts of me that help me eat
and sleep and pee and keep me on this side
of mortality. Kind of like you do, honey.

When I get in bed at night and go to sleep
I always think I'll wake up with you beside me.
And when I'm hurt – joyous, too – the person
who is always next to me has been you.

But there's an elephant in the room now that
needs to be addressed; namely, the big ol' hole
where once I had a chest; that is, until you went
and ripped the heart clean from my breast.

I don't want to beg or plead and this is awkward
at best. But don't you see? You can't leave.
You're part of me. Without you, I can't breathe.

Was That You?

I lay awake at night tortured by my thoughts
thinking of everything that was and was not.
Freud's got nothing on me. I'm my own worst
enemy. That's probably why I can't sleep.

Wind howls outside. Moon climbs high. Inside,
the bed's not right and my mind is a weather
vane in a hurricane. Currents blow it to and fro
and suddenly I hear a knock at the door.

Then all the old memories I hold of you explode
into a dreamlike view and I wonder: Was that you
Sherry Lynn, my old high school crush returned
to tell me you didn't mean to hurt me so much
by going to prom with my best friend then dying
with him later that night on Dead Man's Curve?

Or maybe that was you, my beloved daughter
born of my flesh yet choosing to part with me.
You who put such bitter tears in my eyes.
I loved you and I forgave you; then I had to
set you free. Have you come back to apologize?

Or was it you, Mother? If that's true I still love you
and sorry I wasn't the son you wanted. Did you return
from the land of the dead to tell me no, it wasn't so,
you really cared for me? Because I sat up and thought
I saw you sitting on the chair at the foot of my bed.

And John and Mark or Jeff and Ben. Was it one of you, my
old friends? Did you come back so we could go out again?
I think of those years long ago when our youth was hot
and we were all gung-ho. We ran the bars and howled
at the moon and – not to be rude -- maybe at a girl or two.

Even you who read this poem. Were we once friends
long ago? With each of you, did a deal fall through?
Was there something I didn't do that caused a rift
between you and me to arise? Left a friendship string
untied? Uttered harsh words that wounded your pride?

But most of all and true as sin, ex-wife: I thought
I saw you again. You who kissed my lips and bore
my children, showed me the mysteries of sex and
then gave me the pain of divorce and separation.
Dare I dream you returned to make amends?

I ask myself what did I do that could have caused
such grief in you. And every night I turn out the light
and pay the price by sleeping with solitude, not you.

Oh my loves and all my old friends! If only I knew
the mistakes I made back then I would gladly get on
with life and learn from them. Instead, I lay awake
at night tortured by thoughts of everything that was
and was not. The bed's not right and my mind spins.

Then the wind blows again: first north, then south;
then east, then west; then . . . scattered all about!

I'm Dancing With You Now

Once we were twenty-one with a newborn son
we took pictures of you among old gravestones
in an abandoned pioneer cemetery deep in
the backwoods along the Alabama River.

So happy we were – the three of us -- with all of life
in front of us. You wore your long white cotton dress
because it gave you a ghostly appearance as you stood
among the gravestones at a distance like an apparition
bathed in the river mist; your black hair hung down
your shoulders like Spanish moss on the cypress trees.

We laughed and said what fun it was to recreate one of
those long-lost Southern belles come up from her grave.

You were purposefully mysterious, and I took pictures
to fit the ghostly theme, never dreaming you'd be gone
one day. But here I am lost in memory trying to reach you
across the ages, trying to resurrect you on these pages,
thinking of us when we were twenty-one and poking
around old Cahawba* town down on the Alabama River.

Life hurried on and one day our son was twenty-one.
Meanwhile, we couldn't overcome crummy jobs,
low wages and being worn out from work all the time.
There never was time for life, for living. There wasn't
any money, either. I'm sorry. You changed. I suppose
I did, too. We gradually adopted different points of view.

I started taking angry walks alone after arguments
in which we couldn't get along. We would fight and I
slept in the spare bedroom many nights. I left rooms
when you came in. Turned away when you wanted held.
Wouldn't take dance lessons with you. Let my anger
and resentments ruin too many of our contentments.

Now I stand in the kitchen staring at a bowl of ramen
and remembering when we fixed so much good food.
Always buying fresh produce and eating what we wanted.
At least we agreed on food; I'll say that much for us.

I see my mistakes now how I took our love for granted.
And even though it hurts like so I'm playing the music we
listened to as two drinks sit on the counter. Of course, only
mine gets refilled. I think the drink is just the prompt I need
to get me reeling around the room because a few of those
and I'm light in the step, giddy as heck and dancing with you.

I've got the rhythm and the tune and I've conjured up you.
My lips are hot upon your neck; your scent fills my breath.
You whisper in my ear. I sway and I swing and I think we're
so heavenly, but then I open my eyes and I'm alone.

I'm beset with remorse and regret. I know I'll never get
more chances to get things right with you. Yet here in
this room your phantom image persists perfuming
the very air I breathe while I hold on to you so tight.

I'm sorry I got angry, left rooms, took long walks and
started fights. I wish so hard that I hadn't. But Honey,
would you look at this: I'm dancing with you now.

*Cahawba – First Alabama capital, 1819 -1826. Abandoned
due to flooding.

Moses With Those Damn Tablets

For cryin' out loud. It's Moses come down
from the mountain with those damn tablets
and kiss my ass. We're partying in a Bacchanalia
at the base of the golden calf and he shows up
to tell us pleasure's fleeting and flesh doesn't last.

Then he gives us ten commandments from God above
and says He's the one we should really love. Damn that
Moses! He's looking all holy in a colored robe with a
wooden staff. His hair went white and he's clutching
those freaking tablets and wants no part in our debauch.

What kind of friend is that? He takes the higher ground.
Says he doesn't want to be around for the orgy and that
if it were up to him he'd read us heathens a bible story.
Seriously -- all we want is wine, women, song and sin
but here comes Moses with those damn tablets again!

Moses. Look around. Be reasonable. There's blondes
brunettes and redheads. Some are freaky; others straight.
All will take you to heaven's gate. They like to party and
merry-make. They'll pour you nectar and feed you grapes.

So what say you, Moses? There's nothing here for you to
forsake, nor will we make you climb a hill and talk to a
burning bush. Stay the night with us. Drink some wine.
Sit around the fire and smoke some Hindu Kush.

Man Becomes Hindu God, Destroys Planet

Well it's true. I've blown out my wires. Racing all around my brain
is an electrical fire. It's arcing. It's barking. It's ringing me like a bell.
The voltage and the wattage have fried me all to hell. Which is weird

because I didn't chug a bunch of booze yet I'm feeling really ripped
and I haven't dropped acid since nineteen-seventy-six, but man: Am I
ever on a trip. My poor brain keeps going flippity-flop, then flippity-flip.

And my medulla oblongata's freaking out it can't spell itself anymore,
while my cerebellum and frontal lobe just dashed out the door. You
naughty brain parts need to get back in my head and make me smart
again because I'm sitting in Omaha wondering where my car is parked
and in the meantime you guys flipped me off and took a walk. Thanks.

And holy shit -- look at this! Sparks shoot from my eyes. That's new.
So is the smoke wafting from my ears. It's weird, light-blue and crazy
and I'm not sure what to do. When I breathe, cosmic energy rushes in.

Consider that I twinkled my fingers a minute ago and rain rose to
twenty-thousand feet, then fell and shattered Hong Kong. Don't you
find that a bit much, if not just plain wrong? Or that I wave my arms

and skyscrapers fall, people and all; sneeze and molten snot fireballs
plummet toward Earth; fart and volcanoes blast to life along the
Pacific Rim, throw tons of lava into the sky, wipe out civilization.
Oh I'm one for the ages, all right. And on one of my rampages.

Now, a welding torch burns steady-bright; so, too, does a super nova.
Yet they can't compete with this thing in me that channels universal
energy. But it's in the wrong hands, I tell you, for I am an angry man
shunned all my life, lonely and hungry while others fed with friends.

So Miami, Charleston and Savannah. Throw in Myrtle Beach and Atlanta.
You'll get hurricanes now. Same for you, Norfolk, Virginia. You're just
@#ck-ed. And Kansas, Oklahoma and Nebraska: I'm not even going to
ask you. You're just going up in flames. I don't like your politics or your

football games. That's why I can't ignore your redneck towns.
I'll burn them all down. That's just the way it is. Don't blame me
because you voted the way you did. Is it truly the end of days just
because some poet in Nebraska blew his wires out and thinks he's a
Hindu god? The answer is yes because I gotta do what I gotta do.

We can blame it on a blown fuse if it suits you. But I prefer to go with
Texas Senator Ted Cruz. He really lit my fuse when he shut down the
country reading Green Eggs and Ham. So I'm returning the favor.
Lone Star State -- drought leading to crop failure. And may all the
children of the politicians drink from creeks their parents poisoned.

And San Diego, San Fernando, San Andreas and San Francisco.
I hate to tell you, but you got to go. You get earthquakes because
duh! You live on fault lines, so it's time for you to get schooled.
It's a pity and I already told you: I'm in a really frightful mood.

Neither will you, Kentucky, be so lucky. You'll get a derby, all right, but
it won't be a run for the roses; it'll be a run from the ruins. Thanks to
Mitch McConnell, I'm sending something big and twisty with a funnel
followed by hailing thunderstorms. I'll spin the people round and round.
Some will fall in the cracks. Others get swept away and won't come back.

Missouri, also known as *Misery*, I'm thinking a hundred-and-five
and munching popcorn while you hillbillies struggle to stay alive.
Don't blame me. I can't afford cable TV and have to do something
to keep myself entertained. Besides, you gave us Rush Limbaugh.
That was a sin for which you most certainly must die.

And all you 420 cats in the Pacific Northwest -- Portland, Seattle and
the Hempfest? I'm sick of your bud pics on the Internet. So a pox upon
your gardens and a rot upon your weed. May you all sit and cry watching
your precious buds die while the Feds zero in on your growing activity.

It's not just America. I got a bone to pick with the whole damn world.
Melbourne and Sydney. Hold on tight. I'm sending meteorites.
Timbuktu, you'll be blue when I turn my prides of lions on you.

Madrid? Crawling over you like a giant squid, then smothering your grid.
Singapore? Oh what I have in store for you! Mumbai and Kolkata?
Sending typhoons running through you like knives through butta.

Moscow will have a cow when my freeze brings the Ruskies to their
knees. Folks in Bambesi and Sulawesi: Don't laugh. Things for you won't
be so easy. All the snakes in all your lands will rise and strike you on your
hands. Hanoi and Ho Chi Minh City, Vietnam? Better get in your sampans
and search for dry land. I got a tidal wave and tsunami headed your way.

Malawi, you're getting an owie. Really, Istanbul? You think me a fool?
Here comes a rhinoceros up your Bosporus. We'll see who's cool.
Rome? I'm cracking your dome. Nairobi. You can blow me.

And finally I saved the best for last. Omaha, Nebraska, the town
that ruined me. I'm coming in at ten thousand feet leading a fleet
of B-52s. I think you have a pretty good idea of what I plan to do.
Trust me: I'm going to do to you what you did to me: destroy you.

I know it's a bit odd that our nice little planet will kick the sod
just because my wires got crossed and I got the power of a god.

I mean, go figure, right? Was I harsh, uncompromising and brutal
to ruin the place – a bull in a china shop breaking vases? After all
I did indulge in numerous destructive impulses. But look: it was
like eating the first chocolate in a new box. The joy of destruction
was so great I couldn't stop at just one. You understand that, right?

Besides, mankind wasn't getting anywhere. Century after century.
War and lust and sin and greed with the drama endlessly repeating.
But trust me. I took no comfort in destroying the place. It's just that
the human race had outrun itself. That's why I turned the page.

The Universe Doesn't Care

Son, I know your soul cries out in anguish
at all the mean things it sees in the world.
Mine does, too. We go through hard days
throw our arms up in despair and shout
Life's not fair! We get fired, chewed out
underpaid, arrested and sometimes jailed.

We follow the rules and play it straight
only to discover later cheaters beat us.
Nothing right about it, nothing at all.

But guess what? The universe doesn't care.
In fact, it's the opposite of that. The universe
sets traps everywhere: in the attic, down the hall
and underneath the basement stairs. Watch out.

You must beware of jaws that snap and snares
that catch and tricks that pin the blame on you.
There's work to be done. Don't be someone's prey.

And please don't forget to heed my words of wisdom
because this is a world where little boys get beaten
and lion cubs get eaten. One day you may be bested
by a foe and dragged around on the end of his rope.
I hope not. That's no fate a father wishes for his boy.

Stay on your feet! Thrive. Stay strong and find ways
to survive on this planet where, I hate to suggest it,
mankind is always tested and little girls get molested.

The universe? It plays you foul and it plays you fair
and keeps an ace tucked up its sleeve in case it needs
a spare. And just when you think you've finally gotten
the hang of it all, it calls your bluff and down you fall.

The Way It Is

Some things go on through the ages.
It's no use to try and change them and
these are the things I'm speaking of.

Peace comes on the wings of a dove
Satan with a trident. Checks bounce
when the money's been spent, and
headaches follow merriment.

Money's where they keep it in the banks
and infantry always follows tanks. Itches
always want for scratching and Andrew
always precedes Jackson. What's the thing
they guarantee? Why, your satisfaction!

Checks are always in the mail, not your
pocket, and water drips from the faucet.
Pretty girls hang on rich men's arms, and
wise birds won't fly in violent storms.

Germans celebrate Oktoberfest and
the good beer's made in Munich while
in the harems you'll find the eunuchs.

It's not pretty and it's not the best
but bigger birds push baby brothers
from the nest where they fall down
into jaws of hungry gators to digest.

The liberal arts are dead and gone
and hungry dogs hunt for bones.
Crap flows downhill. Money goes up.
Beggars want you to fill their cup.

Lovers leave partners in the lurch
and don't you know that one hurts.
Oh – and hypocrites go to church.

Daughters grow up and leave their fathers
and when it rains, Mother Earth gets water.
Politicians cheat the people they serve
then turn around and give the rich man
more of what he doesn't deserve. Sorry folks,
shelves are bare, nothing in the store for you.

Hot weather follows cold and when you bust up
shit they mark it sold. It's no use to go insane.
These are things that never change just like
puddin' goes with tain and cornbread with
pork and beans and Mardi Gras in New Orleans.

Now, most folks go to rifle ranges for target practice
just as Mother Earth keeps spinning around on her axis
and at its core the sun burns more than five-hundred
million tons of hydrogen each second. This isn't unusual
nor should it confuse you. It's simply nuclear fusion.

You can swim against the current or you can bend in
the breeze. Friend, the universe doesn't care. When it
acts indifferently and cuts you off at the knees I guarantee
that you can fight it if you wish but it's useless to resist.

So don't ask. Just as dawn breaks on the horizon and
the sun always comes a-rising: that's just the way it is.

I'm No Jew

I'm no Jew. My name is Pugh. I'm Welsh
and nowhere near a Jew. And mom's
a McRoberts so I'm double British Isles:
blond hair, blue eyes. Anglo-Saxon smile.

So some of those Jews look odd to me.
They get wrapped up in their orthodoxy.
Sometimes I drive by them on the street.
The men wearing a single long braid of hair
and wearing their little hats. Dressed all
in black. What's with that? Heck if I know.

I don't understand those things but that's OK
because in spite of my best intentions lots of
things are beyond my mortal comprehension.
And that includes Arabs, Muslims, Hindus
Jews and Seventh Day Adventists. So what?

Do I agree with everything they do? Not really.
But I'm not sure I have to. I don't agree with
everything my wife does but that doesn't mean
I leave her. So I'm no Jew. But I am a veteran.

And I know that if you go to military graveyards
you will see many stars of David among the rows.
I honor those brave men who gave their lives
defeating tyranny and defending democracy.
That's good enough for me. They are my heroes.

In fact, one of my guardian angels is a rabbi
named Herbert Eskin.* He touched my heart
and personified all the best in mankind.
He showed me how to be a better human.

This doesn't mean I like what Jews do in Palestine.
But I have to let that one go because look what
my people did to the red man and the black man.

Neither do I like Bibi Netanyahu who came here
and helped Republicans insult our black president.
Hell no. If you ask me, Bibi's got to go. But look.

I don't like Ted Cruz, Mitch McConnell, Rand Paul
or Tom Cotton. I think they're craven and rotten.
Politicians! They seem to always be so corrupt.
They're everywhere – Russia, America and Israel.

So I truly wish the worst for all the right-wing jerks.
If I were a gypsy witch with a hex I'd send them
a nasty curse. And the best for Sharon Saguy and
Karin Brauner, female warriors in the Pink Front.**
My spirit flies with them wherever they protest.

Jews have their faith, and they have their God.
I have mine, too. In fact, I support religious liberty
and believe the Holy Father grows many branches
on his tree. If one won't work, try another. He gave
us so many ways to reach his heavenly kingdom.

Holy men say heaven is without sex, skin, religion
or gender since we exist there in spirit only. That's
pretty easy to believe. So I don't hate a Jew, AOC
or Omar Ilhan no more than I hate you or me.

That's because we're all human. Therefore, if
I hate someone, I'm hating part of God's creation.
I'm not the brightest. But I hope I'm not that stupid.
That would be a tough one to explain in heaven.

And I'll bet there's a very good chance God could
give me a detention in purgatory for a millennium
or two to reconsider my egotistical attitude.

So I'm no Jew nor Arab, Muslim, Seventh Day
Adventists or Hindu. But I will always stick up
for them because it's the right thing to do.

I leave them be. The street's wide enough

for them and me to live in peaceful harmony.

52

* WW II Army combat chaplain and Detroit rabbi.
Read his story, "Rabbi, Teach Us!" at ganja-tales.com/stories
** Israeli protest group largely comprising female artists
protesting Bibi Netanyahu and political corruption.

Father Pain, Part I

Father Pain, I've read that suffering
is the footstool of divinity and that
without a hurt the heart is hollow.

By those measures, then, I reckon I'm
downright saintly and my heart's full
of joy because you ripped my wings off

when you shoved me down those stairs
and landed me with a snap, crack and pop
into your domain: The Kingdom of Pain.

You broke my left arm, then went down on me
taking out both bones below my right knee.
Tibia? Fibula? Flaming torches, Roman candles.

Like a fighter pilot pulling g's I grunted and
strained to get you off me, to keep you at bay.
Yet you were so determined to have your way.

I even fled to unconsciousness to escape you but
you chased me and dragged me back to your ring
of suffering so you could keep doing your thing
cuffing my chops and knocking my block off with
savage precision and monstrous rhythm although
I was on my knees begging you not to please.

Yet you ticked and tocked until I went white in shock.
You wiped my slate clean. You erased my everything.
You fit me to a spit and slow-roasted me in agony.

That's why I pray I never feel you again. And I'll be first
to admit: you won. Therefore, I bow to you Father Pain.
When you were done with me I was wiped out, through.
And I now know for sure who the boss is — it's you!

Father Pain, Part II

(for Jenny)

Father Pain, a moment ago I was fine.
Now I'm fighting for my life. I've always
heard of you and wondered what I'd do
if you came around. Well, here we are.

My God! You hurt so much. Seriously,
I'm on a morphine drip and you're still
killing my shit thrashing me relentlessly
in such a vicious feeding frenzy. I get it.

I'm just your dinner, a hunk of meat and
you're a Great White dragging me off in
your bloody jaws. I scream, writhe, twist
and cry: "I can't take any more of this!"

But then, that's your great lesson, isn't it,
Father Pain? You taught me that I could.

Staring At The Hospital

I heard the whoosh of Death's scythe
and ducked just in time as it whistled
by and took my top knot yet left my
head still attached to my shoulders.

So now I stand in the parking lot
grateful to have my life back and
for no more painful IVs, bright lights
noisy machines and rude employees
who could care less if I sleep or not.

Looking at all the rows of windows to
all those rooms I say a prayer for those
of you stuck in your beds, hurt, confused
or filled with sickness, regrets or gloom.

If you're dying too soon I hope your spirit
and you have made amends. Even more
than that, I pray pain doesn't play with you
and make you grind your teeth and clutch
the sheets begging for relief, as I did.

When the lights dim and the violins play
your final refrain, may you find sweet grace
in the closing notes. May love touch your heart.
God will take your hand and guide you across.

Trying To Get Out Of The Hospital

Those doctors. They sure are a funny bunch.
They came by my bed this morning, said Hi,
How ya doing? I replied: Are you kidding?

You didn't see me pole-vaulting the Omaha VA
at daybreak when you were driving to work
or jumping over cars in the parking lot or
somersaulting down Forty-Second Street?

Because before that I hurdled the Bob Kerry
Bridge across the Missouri River, dashed
over to Iowa and leapfrogged all the way
to the Bayliss Fountain in Council Bluffs.

Isn't that enough to get me out of here?

Death Answered The Door

I went to see Fred yesterday
but Death answered the door.
He said: *Come on in, friend.*

I said I'm here to see Fred.

Death said: *Forget Fred. He dead.*
I peeked in and sure enough
there was Fred, lying on the floor.

I said Oh shit! I'm not next, am I?

Death grabbed me by my shirt
threw me up against the wall
rolled his reptilian fist into a ball
under my chin and uttered forth
with foul breath this admonition.

That all depends, he said, *on who
you are. Are you a mighty oak
who defies the storm to stand
with the tallest trees? Or are you
a little sapling toppled by a breeze?*

*Are you the brave man who stands
up to the bully? Or do you cower down
before him shaking in your knees?*

*Do you jump in the ring and say
I can do it! Then carry the prize home?
Or did you take a pounding to the bone?*

*Do you sit on the side of the road crying
woe is me and boo-hoo-hoo? Or do you
get up and do what you have to do?*

Are you made of iron, not tin? Can you
play a winning hand and not fold your cards in?
Because I need a warrior, not a worry wort.

A fighter, a good sport. A man who would be king.
Not a light-weight, a weakling or a gelding.
I'm talking about a boxer, a pit bull, a rabid dog
who chews off my leg. Not a whiney bitch who begs.

Listen to me close now, he said. *You humans get*
too many choices in life, if you ask me. Some false
others true. But the biggest one you have to make
is who are you? Now, do you still want to come in?
If you can and you have a plan I'll leave you alone.
But if you don't, I'm dragging your sorry ass home.

I smacked his fist from off my chest and stared hard
into his eyes before replying: "Hell yes, Mister Death.
I am in fact that guy." And then I stepped inside.

The Devil Turned The Thermostat Down

Come gather far and gather near, for I've got a story
to tell. The Devil turned the thermostat down in hell.
No really. Satan said: *You bitches worked hard enough
and did your stuff okay so I'm giving you a break today.*

Suddenly the sulphur stench dissipated and dissolved.
Fresh air rushed in, replacing the awfully normal smell.
Of course, everyone in hell said no way Satan would
let them play, that his was just one of his tricks and
they'd be damned if they'd fall for it and have to pay.

(Of course, being in hell, they already were damned,
but that's beside the point.)They weren't going for it.
But they did enjoy the sudden drop in temperature.

As you suspected, Satan's reaction wasn't pleasant.
He got kicked out of heaven and doesn't do well with
rejection. He bellowed and roared and stomped on
the ground, then swung his mighty whip around and
and around before bringing it down on a bitch's back.
And for good measure, another crack on top of that.

And then was heard wails from the pit of despair
down there where doomed souls trudge around in
a circle chained to the pole that grinds their soul.

How they scratch on their itches from the clap and vd
and all the rest of the sexually transmitted diseases
their foul bodies all covered with boils and lesions.
Lifting their bales of what-ifs, toting their barges of
coulda-beens. Hoisting their sails on the lake of regrets.

Others moaned and groaned and strained their backs
while pushing cart after cart of their sins up the track.
And Lord it was hot – hot as, well, Hell. And everything
reverted to the same shitty mess it had always been.
The gnashing of teeth. Sounds of snarling beasts. And

Satan said: *Dammit all to hell. This is something
I really can't explain. I could pave the walls with gold
down here and these bitches would still complain.
And that's why I keep 'em locked up in their chains.*

The Last Bowl

(for Steve)

Gosh dang it! I told myself this bowl of
Blueberry Blast would last until after
dinner. That was going to be the deal.

But I just ate my lunch and can't think of
anything better than a puff of good bud
after that grilled-cheese sandwich I just slayed.

I must admit before I ate I took a few tokes to
stimulate my appetite. Then before that, the blues
came 'round, so you know what I had to do.

As for waking up today, that took a hit or two.
Now sonofabitch! Would you look at this?
I'm out of weed again. Now what am I gonna do?

A Nebraskan Visits Colorado

I told my Ma and I told my Pa I'm tired of this here Omaha.
Denver, Denver is the show. That is where I want to go.
They got legal weed out there people say is beyond compare.
Ma and Pa said "Have you lost your mind? Stay away from it!"

I replied: "Are you kidding me? Have you ever tried that shit?
It's fantastic. Lifts your spirits, calms your nerves, helps you
through life's tight curves." Ma and Pa just wrung their hands and
cried: "Oh boy of ours. We thought we raised you to know better!"

Then they really sounded the alarm. Pa said: "Sonny Boy, we only
want joy for you but at this minute we've got chores to do and
you're needed on the farm. Once we get the corn crop in we
figured you'd drive to Lincoln and Husker-up with Go Big Red!

I just shook my head. Lincoln? I remember from history that he
famously debated Horace Greeley who said: "Go West young man."

So I went to Interstate Eighty on my thumb, got a ride with a fellow
cannabis pilgrim driving from Missouri. He said: "I'm headed to Denver
to smoke me some good weed" to which I replied: "Amen, Brother,
that's what we need!" He had a joint and I had one, too; and after we
smoked 'em up I shut my eyes for a few and I woke up in Denver town.

Man I love that mountain air! Smells like skunk buds everywhere.
Walked into my first shop and thought it was the jungle because
a Grape Ape got all in my business, claiming he was king of all the
cannabis sativas. He picked me up and threw me down and when
I hit the ground a White Rhino let out a blast of THC and ran over me.

When I awoke I ate a banana, but it was kush. And I won't beat around
the bush. That Banana Kush kicked me in the touché. The tangerines
were no better. They put me in a Tangerine Haze, which was a really
dreamy Neptunian phase of chilling out with little cupids flying about.

Next place featured Sour Tsunami, which was great for my anxiety
but in all honesty it rolled right over me. I held my breath and shut my
eyes as it took me down in a very deep dive but then it was like whoa –
I began seeing things I didn't want to see. I told myself: *By thunder!*

Don't let that tsunami drag you under! And when I crawled out I was
on Maui Wowie, a tropical island topped with pineapple candy and
a bouncy, creative high. I ain't lying: I thought that was fine and dandy.

But then I went a step too far when I took a hit of Death Star, which
shot me past the moon and Mars and put me floating in space with
asteroids and shooting stars. That was a bit much for me. I'm content
to watch the galaxy through a telescope, which is what I hope to do
once I find my way out of this crystal palace where garden gnomes are
giving away ice-cream cones topped with capitate-stalked trichomes.

Seeking to get earthbound with edibles, I ate some chocolate-infused
incredibles but they added too much fuel to my trajectory once again
so I had to go for another spin around the planet. That's when I threw
the towel in to get back to good-old, solid-old, boring-ass Nebraska.

Now I'm in Omaha smoking gack weed watching corn grow down by
the Mighty Mo. No, it's not Denver, nor so much fun. But I do sit
in Omaha wondering how people in Colorado get anything done!

We're Here To Help You Write

It's true you got a lot of poetry in you
but it don't express so easy which is
why we're going to help you get it out.

We're gonna pry you open with a crowbar
and boil you in water with the fruit jars.

Open you like a can of juice and mix you
in the blender, then truss you up like a
beer-butt chicken or the Christmas goose.

All of this will of course make you play fast
and loose with your words until you get
into the swing of your nuance and meaning.

So we're sure you'll understand when we
hold you upside down like a piggy bank and
shake you by your heels until you squeal and
all your poems come tumbling out of you.

If that won't do the trick and flush them out
we're gonna bust you in your lip and mouth
before we knock your teeth out to give you pain.

Maybe that will help you gain you a poem.
If not, we'll roast you in a 500-degree oven
so you can write about heat before we open
your vein and corkscrew our way into your brain
so we can try and explain what makes you tick.

Honestly, please think nothing of it when we
sock you in the eye, hang you out to dry and
slice you up for stir fry. There's no extra charge
and our bill won't be large because we honestly
really and truly are here to help you write. Get it?

Down On The Farm

Katie didn't bar the door
so All Hell broke loose and
tore up the pea patch, then
ripped off to the back forty
and started raised Cain.

We sent for help but it never
came. So Daddy quit tendin'
his liquor still and grabbed
him a jug to find All Hell so
he could bend him to his will.

He snatched All Hell by his neck.
Pried his jaw open and poured
down the shine. Now what do
you know? Hell's wobblin' outta
town all snockered and half-blind.

My Daddy is one tough man. Eats
nails for breakfast with slabs of Spam
while guzzling coffee from a gas can.

If he rolls in the bar and says you're
sitting in his chair, you best get up or
or he'll beat you down right there.

Teeth!

Lord, I keep trying to have a good day
but you keep knocking my teeth out.
What's with that? I try and be your
faithful servant. Say my prayers and
be observant of your ways. But then
I go to the dentist and get slayed.

Not to get Biblical, but I'm actually
so dismayed I've taken to gnashing
and wailing my teeth. It's beyond
belief how my bicuspids got busted.

Plus my grinders don't chew, nor do
my munchers crunch much anymore.
And I've had so many bridges, crowns
and root canals my mouth looks like
the dikes and canals on the Zuider Zee.

Then time goes by. Days turn to weeks.
And what do you know? I keep losing
teeth, which I can't figure out because
I'm a vegetarian and don't eat meat!

All I know is if I lose another molar
I'm absolutely going to go bipolar.
Lord, why do you treat me this way?

A Vegetarian At Thanksgiving

Really? You want me to eat a bird?
I find the very notion quite absurd.
As for things that oink and squeal
I could never make a pig a meal.
And veal? My heart breaks in half
to see people eating baby calves.

So no ma'am and no sir! Put the ham
back in the can as far as I'm concerned.
I'll also pass on the wild boar or venison
as well as that loin chop or brisket.

I'm fine staring at bottles of wine and
cider standing beside bowls of stuffing
mashed potatoes and gravy, cranberries
baked apples and cauliflower casserole.
There's also green beans, roasted carrots
vegetable soup, wild rice and yeasted rolls.

Indeed, these things do suffice to contain
my delight; unless of course you may wish
to tempt me with a big-ol' slice of that
awesome chocolate bourbon pecan pie!

Frog's Lament

Spiders, worms, larvae -- even small fish.
These are my favorite things, although
once I dined on finer fare than bugs; in fact,
I recall drinking wine from porcelain jugs.

Then one day a sorceress put a witch's hex
upon my golden crown of hair and all of me
that once was fair turned into an ugly mess.
A frog, no less! With a lumpy mug for a face.

Disgraced, I was. And doomed to hop about
the kingdom I once ruled. You know how
the story goes. Only a kiss from a true love
now can stop me from being a toad.

Now you know why my heart carries such
a heavy load and how a sorceress's curse
dispersed me to this group of diverse, tailless
largely carnivorous short-bodied amphibians

otherwise known as frogs where – oh my gosh! –
I sit around croaking on moss-covered logs
staring at things with my bulging eyes while
trying not to notice my slimy mucous-like skin.

In the meantime, I've eaten a snail, a minnow
a slug a bug and a fly. And they tasted fine.
Now I'm looking for ganja leaves. You see:
weed gives me consolation at my plight.
I chew it a bit and get high waiting as I do
for my true love to come passing by.

Scorpion

Really? You want to step in the ring with me?
Haven't they told you how I fight so angrily?
How my sting is so sharp and how I love to hear
people scream. Haven't they told you these things?

How I rear my tail high in a deadly arc and plunge it
quick into a quivering heart; or, clasping victims
in my claws, pick them apart slowly -- nose to foot,
chin to bum -- carefully not missing a single crumb?

Or lungs, for that matter. They're good. A liver or two.
And I particularly like brains -- yum! So I ask again:
Haven't they told you any of these things? *Girtab,*

Sumerians called me: *The Stinger* who scared Phaeton
hauling the sun, making him scorch Africans. Later I
stung Orion who flees me still, dashing out of sight
below the horizon when I rise in the sky to slay him.

Strong I am, sleek and powerful and plotting with
dark, penetrating eyes. I seek nothing less than
total possession. Ruled by Mars, planet of death
and fighting, I find these activities rather exciting.

Please don't think me wicked, vicious or mean.
I'm just being myself. I was hard-wired this way,
one of many born into a world, just as you were,
where I had to defend myself or be eaten alive.

I, too, had to learn to survive, to be the fighter
in the ring with a trident and bloody net sweeping
the sand seeking to trip a hapless fellow's feet.

So if you want to step in the circle with me
bring a sharp sword, a sharp sword, indeed.
For the game I play is a death match.
Only one of us gets out of here alive.

Rabbit Talks To Fish About Her Wiggle

(for Stephanie)

Today's a very pretty day so rabbit has come out
to play. She hops along the flowing stream and
puts her nose in for a drink whereupon she sees
Fish, who swims over for a visit and says: Hi Rabbit.

But what's this? Rabbit's perplexed. Fish,
she says, is someone down in the dumps today?
Has a certain fish lost her swim and her sway –
the cute little way she sashays through the water
trolling her tail and showing a Mona Lisa smile?
You feeling okay or are you under water today?

Well Rabbit, you're right. I don't know what's come
over me. I used to swim around the deep blue sea
but all of a sudden I'm the picture of despondency.
My tail is weak, my fins are sore and I have no desire
to bat my big round eyes or puff out my gills anymore.

In fact, I'm so blue I should be a bluegill, not a bass.
And I'm not very happy. I feel so crappy I might as well
be a crappie. One with cramps. A crappie with cramps.
You see, I make bad choices when it comes to fish men.
I throw a good flirt and flash a cute fin, then follow them
into their dens and before I know it . . . fish eggs again.

Oh Fish, I'm sorry to hear your woeful greeting. First,
remember to count your blessing that you haven't
been caught and eaten. You've just got a bad case of
the wounded-fish wiggle. Therefore, we'll get you
rehabilitated so you won't end up as shark bait or
else as the main entree on someone's dinner plate.

Now, I thought we had this talk before about how
you dance along the ocean floor and move your body
to the rhythm and motion and music of the waves.
But I see that we need to have it again because
once more you swam out and got your heart broken.

So look here, girl. Do you rock and do you roll?
Do you strut and do you stroll? Can you be all coy
and shy? Can you catch a lover's eye? I'm a bunny
so I hop but you're a fish so you flip and flop.

But just stop, would you, before you get the urge
to wiggle like a wounded damn fish? That wounded
fish wiggle is awful body language that puts you at a
disadvantage. Strength and confidence are what you
want to project, not weakness and indecisiveness.

They're too abject. Puff up your chest. Swim with zest.
Get out in front of your school of fish. Be strong inside.
It's okay to show some tail but flash it once and swim on
down the trail. Get it? Make *them* chase after you.

That's the way to find an aqua mate you'll be happy
to copulate with, to swim around and lay eggs with.
Got it? Good. Now don't you dare forget it!

Organ Grinder's Sad Song (I Lost My Mojo)

I lost my monkey, but I'm trying to get him back.
That furry little flunky done jumped the track.

I set out searching for him and I'll be damned.
I caught him in a strip joint knocking back gin
and stuffing bananas in a girl chimp's G-string.
I said: "Mojo, where you been? Come on back."

Mojo (agitated, hopping around) scratched his pits
and said: "Why, I been playing the ponies in Omaha
at AK-SAR-BEN." I got up to grab him but off he ran
to New Orleans. So I hitched up my Missouri mules
and flew down South like a gosh-darn fool. Searching
up and searching down, I found him in Cajun Town
inside Madam LaRue's getting a she-ape tattoo!

"Mojo," I says, "Just come on back. I'll make sure
you always have snacks. Just don't get your nose
out of joint." He huffed up, said the hell he won't
then scampered to the railroad track and hopped
a train to Belmont where he bet on a nag he thought
would run fast. But Mojo lost his monkey ass!

I'm glad. Teach him a lesson. That damn chimp.
I gave him everything he has. Without me he's just
another monkey picking off fleas. With me? Stability.
Plus, a purple velvet vest with a jaunty matching cap
and plenty of yams to eat. If the issue is more peanuts
I'll give him the whole sack. Fewer working hours?
I'll cut them back. Bananas? He can have the whole
bunch. The point is this: I'm nothing without Mojo.

People don't want to see an old man grinding an organ
or squeezing an accordion. They want Mojo, not me.

Without Mojo, I have no relevancy. By Jiminy!
I'm trumped by a chimp! What's with that?

Yet I do miss the scampering of his little feet.
Mojo's no lamb and he's certainly no sheep
but he's still the beast I want to keep. Oh Mojo!
Come shuffle across the floor for me waving
your hands back and forth down by your knees.

Or jump upon the table top and steal a sip of my tea
you who has a flea or two . . . okay, maybe three.
Who's counting? Not me. I'm just eager to see you
ditty-bop or monkey strut or maybe do a jig.

That I could dig. You can call me a lunatic, a halfwit
or even a dumb twit, but I'm willing to dismiss all
your faults if only we could reconnect. I've thought
this through and through and hate to admit it but
the fact is I'm just a lonely old man without you.

Junk Mail

Cindy says I'm cute and don't have to be alone and Rachel
promises Crazy Love Over The Phone. Moira wonders where
I've been and Hot and Bothered is waiting for a reply, while
Mary Beth wants to know why I haven't responded to her
request and Francesca Jewels says she knows I like her best.

Hortense, meanwhile, mails me incessantly, and Candace
craves intimacy. Janet promises Things Dark And Naughty.
And Vicky Daudet needs sex today. I hope that poor girl
gets laid. Me? I'm waiting for a Certified Letter from my
Quicken Loans Partner for my 10K Payday. Meanwhile

I'm Cutting the Fat quite well now that the Hernia Surgical
Mask has come to hold back My Leaky Gut just in time for me
to Manage My Depression for Better Bedroom Performance
on the Keto Diet and CBD Goodies Mary Jane promises me.

If not, I'll get that Injury Claim going for my Prostate Recovery
so I Can Feel More Alive by reviving My Sexual Health at the
Raging Bull Casino thanks to the Insta-Hard Partner I purchased
at CVS Pharmacy to guarantee no woman will ever leave me.

And thank god for that warranty on the Male Elongator which
Keeps Them Coming Back For More. Which reminds me, I need
to get a Power Bolt for my toolbox, along with America's Flashlight,
which I can use to find My Injury Advocate who's going to help me
Have It All topped off with I'll Never Have To Pay A Bill Again and

I can Eliminate Morning Wood. So it's all good. I actually ordered
some Get Rock Hard because Francesca's invited me into the Love
Warrior's Circle tonight. Good thing I had the foresight to order the
Get My Breath Back Oxygen Concentrator FedEx Express. I have the
feeling after I go through my junk mail I'm going to be out of breath.

The Writer's Dog

Runs all day and half the night.
Lungs are big, legs are strong.
Master's dead. Dog has no home.

He runs in Master's place instead.
Pulls Master's sled full of his stories.

Dog hauls those words. North Star
shines overhead. Dog trots ever on,
undeterred: steady, steady as he goes.

Makes his bed in the freezing snow.
Curls up and sleeps alone. Gets up
at dawn and runs again all day long.

Along the trail in a sunlit forest
ice glistens in the air and sled rails
whisper softly over fresh snow.

Wolf tracks. Bear follows. Eagle calls.
The Writer's Dog outruns them all.
Steadfast. Determined. Resolved.

Juneau, Anchorage, Fairbanks, Nome.
He is going to bring them poems.
Jack Frost brings with him quite a shiver
but Dog won't stop till the words delivered.

The Runny Cup

Oh yes! Life kept filling me up. I said
thank you, sir. That's quite enough.

Life said: *No, you haven't had enough.*
It poured and poured and gave me more
than I could handle. I cried: Enough! but
Life said: *No, here 'tis a little more* and
filled me all the way up to the brim.

And oh how my emotions bubbled and
brewed and steamed and stewed in
my heart as if it were a mighty ocean
in which a storm had suddenly blown up.

Love and hate and anger and sin were just
a few of my fiery passions that splattered
and splashed and sloshed all over the rim.

And again I said to Life: Sir, I must protest!
Life only laughed in jest before replying:
In vain, Sir. For I gave you my very best!

Oh no you didn't, I cried. Life, I sought relief
from you and all I got was grief. I tried and
tried, then tried some more and each time
you knocked me down to the floor. Oh sure.

You filled me up. Yet paradoxically, I never
had enough because I couldn't hold you in.
And now you've left me with this runny cup.

What Else Did You Need To Know?

I'm the stick that stirs your drink.
The plunger that unclogs your drain
and all the bubbles in your champagne.

I'm the burning sun who makes you grow.
The flame shooting out your afterburner.
A racing car screeching around your corner.

I'm the freezing cold that makes it snow.
I'm Orion, Rigel and the Southern Cross.
The Man, *El Hefe*, the Dude and the Big Boss.

The activator, the originator, the creator
the one who gets the job done. Now,
what else did you need to know?

Advice To My Son On Drinking

Son, if one tastes good, two are better.
When it comes to drinking you got to be
a go-getter. So pound them down and
drink them up. I toast to your health and
bid you strength when you lift your cup.

Two are better – that's for sure. But after that
how about three or four? You know: Jack and
Johnny and Tom and Jerry? They're the friends
with whom we make merry. Then Alexander
with the brandy and don't forget Bloody Mary.

Honestly, there's so much booze to choose from.
Get up off the sofa. Go out and get your drunk on.
Ain't no one else gonna do that drinking for you
and good things don't come your way for free.

Work hard to drink your fill. Don't worry if you
run up a bill. The fun begins when you get past
ten and Katie comes to bar the door. Make sure
then when weak-kneed ones are on the floor that
you're the one slamming mai tais and martinis.

Don't forget that you weren't raised in quicksand
and ants fall down where giants stand. That's why
when it comes to drinkin' you got to be a man.
Get on your barstool way up high and take a dive
into the Whiskey River. Be a fish swimming in it.

Down the hatch, here she comes -- another shot
of bourbon. And don't worry if your panties get
all twisted up in knots because when it comes
to drinking, winners always show up two-fisted.

Go ahead and be a fool. Ride to Moscow on a mule.
And if someone beats you to the liquor trough
make damn sure you knock him off because *it's*

Kam pai! and drain your glass. Roll around drunk
and bust your ass. *Skoal! and Prosit*! and *Salud!*
to you. Cheers! and Good Health! and Mud In
Your Eye, Too. First one's on me, second's on you.

Fill 'em up and toss 'em down again, then switch
over from vodka to gin. And before you fade away
in a hazy mist, don't forget to kiss Jose. Why's that?

He's the one who brought all the tequila. Got it?
That's the way. Trust me on this. There is no other
because brother, you're either drinking or you're not.

And remember this: counting drinks is for pussies
and wussies, and rehab's for quitters. And son, you
ain't no wuss. And you damn sure ain't no quitter.
Oh hell no. Not you. I raised you better than that.
Because when it comes to drinkin', you're a go-getter.

Poetry Rehab

When I was an alcoholic I kept my booze close by
for comfort. A bottle in a boot. A pint in a shoe.
A fifth in the basement and quart in the closet
behind the broom. My whiskey well never ran dry.

Relief: that's what liquor brought me. And a warm
drunken haze to help me make it through my days.
Then my wife left me, saying AA or no more her.

So I joined the circle and held hands while reciting
the Lord's Prayer and like everyone else when I
introduced myself said my name, then added that
I was an alcoholic. I tried my best to climb the steps

and by God, over the months, I climbed all twelve
of them one-by-one and sobered up. It wasn't easy.
I had to admit I had a problem bigger than I was
and couldn't handle it alone; that I needed help.

I did so well at all the steps I discovered another
one: a Thirteenth Step, if you will. And boy was I
surprised to see it was poetry. It's just crazy that
when I got off the booze I discovered a verse or
two and the more I read the deeper in I got.

So now a bunch of odes are strewn about my abode
and I never fear because I keep Shakespeare near.
I no longer listen to the itty bitty shitty committee in
my head that tells me I need to drink myself dead. No.
I quit my stinkin' thinkin' when I finally quit drinkin'.

I keep a sonnet in my sock and a poem in my pocket.
Relief is what they bring me. And a warm, loving wife
to help me through my days because she came back
when I graduated from AA. Yet I still stand in a circle

hold hands with fellow penitents and miscreants and
say the Lord's prayer. But this time they're literary
miscreants. So after I introduce myself, just like
everyone else, I say: "And I am a poetry-holic."

The Black Hole Of Addiction

Go on, then. Get your nose in it.
Get your snoot full and your belly
too. Smoke it up. Drink it down.

Or take a walk through porno town.
Snort some coke, shoot some dope.
Go throw some dice at the casino.

Have affairs. Drive too fast.
Always look for a dopamine blast.

Try to come to terms with the craving
need you have to feed the hole inside
of you that never can be fed enough.

Poor thing: you always overstuff for
wanting too much. We watch you
consume it, and it consume you.

My Mouth And My Guts

My Mouth said: *Man, this sure tastes good.*
My Guts replied: *Slow down and take it easy*!

My Mouth said: *Keep eating. Don't listen to old
Grumpy Guts down there. He's a party pooper.*
My Guts replied: *Boy, are you going to be sorry.*

Mouth pretended not to hear, so My Guts got
indignant at the snub. *How do you like that?*
he mused. *I've been waiting for him down here
on the bottom end of things, but that bloody fool
thinks he's going to rule. He forgot he won't get
any relief until he lets me speak my piece.*

Then — to remind My Mouth who's first, not last --
My Guts let out a furious blast of gas and said:
*By the way. Not to be an asshole about it, but
there's one point on which I'd like to correct* you:
I'm not a party pooper. I'm just a pooper.

Charon Speaks

The river Styx flows fast and wide
but I will take you to the other side.
Rowing is the job I do for those of you
whose lives are through. Sorry you're in
the boat. Worry not. We'll soon be afloat.

Yes, some take my ride; others get wings.
For you there'll be no heavenly things.
And please don't bother with those tears.
My heart's been hardened over the years.
Besides, tears mean nothing down here
for those of you whose lives are through.

Please don't ask where we're headed for.
Have you never heard of Hell's Trap Door?
It gives you quite a ride as you may imagine.
You tumble and fall for so many fathoms.

As to where you'll land, it's hot as heck.
What did you think you were going to get?
You'll be in the Mohave, the Gobi or Sahara
howling with goblins and burning in despair.

Save your prayers. And your bribes, too.
Money means nothing down here for those
of you whose lives are through and where
Master Pluto rules in dread and eternal fear.

To cry out now: *It's not too late for me!* would be
a cliché. When you should have worked, you played.
Now you must pay the wages for all of your sins.

These smooth-worn oars feel good in my hands
when I put in my back and pull away from the land.

Rowing is the job I do for those of you whose lives
are through. And ladies, please cover that leg. As for
that breast? There's none to beg. Such things mean
nothing down here. You will see as we draw near.

I'm a boatman, not an academian to lecture you on
morals and rectitude, but shouldn't you have been
reading scripture or vowing yourself to some noble
pursuit rather than hopping in and out of beds in
your birthday suit? You went ahead and got laid but
I guess you forgot that owls hoot and pipers get paid.

Too bad, so sad your life was a disaster and now I must
bring you to my Master who bids me row all the faster.
Indeed, business is brisk today but it's always this way.

Here's the mother shore where you step out so I can
return for more. Sure, karma's a bitch! Did you never
hear it? That's how you got here. No point trembling in
fear. You actually paid for your spot over all your years.

The River Styx flows fast and wide and you have come
to its dark side. That something in your eye? You seem
to be rubbing it. Here's my handkerchief. You can use it
to wave goodbye as I row away and leave you behind.

Autumn

Finally the leaves must surrender
to a will far greater than their own
desire to dance on limb and bough.

With timid tumbles and cautious flips
they commit themselves from the heights
nervously uncertain of the seed's promise.

Here We Are Again

It's okay, Mister Vladimir Putin.
Go ahead, start all the looting.
Kill all the men, rape the women.
Get started on ethnic cleansing.

There's no need to get in a haste.
The West will stand by and watch
as you grind Ukraine into paste.

Sarajevo, Aleppo and Ukraine.
The end result is always the same:
death, misery, suffering and pain.
Politicians playing their games.
Innocents fed into the flames.

* For Tetiana Perebyinis and her children,
Mykyta, 18; and Alisa, 9; and church volunteer
Anatoly Berezhnyi, 26; who was helping them
cross a bridge. All killed by a mortar round in Irpin,
Kyiv, March 11, 2022.

War Dogs

The war dogs are howling for meat.
More bodies are what they want to eat.
They stay very well fed indeed because
they're always feasting on our dead.

You can see all the graves in a row.
So many exist, yet more always grow.
And of course we all know the reason
they died was the war dogs had to eat.

So come all you mothers and come
all you fathers. Give us your sons and
give us your daughters because the
war dogs are hungry for meat. See how
they demand to be fed; to turn us living
into the dead. It's madness to live like
this, but they've got nothing else instead.

It's always the same story about honor
and glory with those who start the war.
And all along their only motive was profit:
to make the stock market soar. That's why
they clamor for more children for slaughter.

Do you hear the war dogs howling, then,
down in the fires of Hell and the domain
of the dead? They want more children.
It's flesh by the pound they desire.
They're demanding to be fed now.

The Boys In The Trenches Want A Poem

The boys in the trenches want a poem.
Something with truth and beauty to
inspire them. They're so tired of war
of being stuck in trenches with thousands
of stinking men listening to the wounded
and dying crying in No Man's Land at night.

Then when the sun comes up, going out to
thrust a bayonet into a fellow human being's
guts, mow them down with machine-guns
or blast survivors to bits with mortars and
hand-grenades. It's awful business and deep
inside, angels cry and spirit knows something's
wrong with all this brutality and killing.

So the boys in the trenches have had it with war
and want to go home -- home to the old farm;
home to their girls with their sweet-loving arms
for rolling in the hay, beers at the bar, picnics
in the yard and fields of wheat that need cut.

All these things sound like good deals to the boys
in the trenches who just want something beautiful
and real, but most of all don't want to come home
in a bag with a flag for their wives and children
reduced to a sad memory and a picture on the wall.

You see: the boys in the trenches no longer believe
the lie that they are the ones who must die for causes
concocted by crooked politicians who never served
and corporations, private contractors and profiteers.

And that's why the boys in the trenches want a poem.
A poet will tell them the truth. A poet they can trust.
Crooked politicians and corporations? Not so much!

You Can See It In Their Faces

You can see in their faces how eager they are
to please, to earn treats from Master; how they
love authority, a firm hand and a strong command.

They can't think, don't want democracy. Salute
smartly. Take a knee to pledge loyalty to The Leader.
Enamored with power. Don't care about others.

Favor harsher punishments, longer sentences and
seizing malcontents to be sent to for-profit prisons,
thus filling donor pockets and pleasing rich investors.

Don't ask questions. Rig elections. Collude with Russia.
Sell out America. Suspicious and clever. Mistresses.
Sweaty upper lips, secret services and private eyes
to cover up their shady deals, intrigues and dirty lies.

Court-packers, preyers of weak minds wagging their
cunning tongues to twist facts and convince fools to
keep drinking the potion they pedal that ruins lives.

Oh those rouges and cheaters and double-dealers!
You can see in their faces how they'll do what they're
told: sign a death warrant from The Leader just like
falling off a log, then light a cigarette and tell an NCO:
"You have your orders. Now go and shoot the dog."

And how amazing is it that they always have what
The Leader needs? Axes to chop off traitors' heads?
You bet. Sandbags for the execution pits? Got 'em
right here along with spools of thread to sew lips shut
so truth can't speak nor voices sing; hence, scapegoats
must be lined up so they can swing on the end of ropes.

We the people see all of this in the reptile faces of the
back-stabbing betrayers and crooked politicians willing
to bash in someone's head if The Leader says do it.

We know Lady Liberty's seen better days and that we
must defend the honor of our fallen dead, our bravest
of the brave who gave their lives for better than this
insurrectionist mess. Which is why we pray for strength
and the courage to make America a decent place again.

And what of this test on our democracy today? I wonder
what history will say of the time when freedom in America
almost got stolen away? I know what I have to say:

You could see it in their faces, how eager they were to please,
to earn treats from master. How they loved authority, a firm
hand and a strong command. And mostly, you could see how
they despised democracy, embraced tyranny and sold their
souls to a Russian devil in exchange for Kremlin gold.

We Did Not Die For This!

"A house divided against itself cannot stand."
Abraham Lincoln, 1858.

Matt caught a bullet in his throat while
a mortar shell blew Mike and Jim and Joe
to smithereens inside the boat. I was shot
in the eye and couldn't see Dick and Jim
trying to stuff their guts back in along
the bloody beach that day at Normandy.

Scared stiff, we nonetheless charged out
into the face of death, fought our way
to the tree of liberty and bled out on it.
Kids, none of us over 20. Gave our lives
so that you reading this could live free.

So the dust of our bones was greatly disturbed
in the hallowed ground where we're interred
in the American cemetery at Luxembourg
when we heard news of traitors running loose
in the halls of our people's house in Congress.

We all rose up and cried: We did not die for this!
For a rabid mob to smash the doors and loot.
To attempt to shoot the Speaker of the House
and hang the Vice President of the United States.

To watch a capitol policeman dragged down steps
and beaten to death by so-called patriots? No sir!
We didn't sacrifice our lives on freedom's altar
so that could occur. The very notion is absurd.
We died to keep you and your descendants free.

That's why as for that mess on January the sixth
in Washington, D.C. we fallen sons of liberty rise up
and in our loudest voices cry: We did not die for this!

2022, A Requiem

Man fell from his grace.
Eve covered her face.
Adam's also disgraced
for leading her astray.

The sun's off course.
Phaeton's horses ran wild.
His father's chariot lies in ruin
along the fiery way and Apollo
hastens to scold his errant child.

Sagittarius missed her mark.
Alas, her arrow fell in the dark.
Without a torch to light man's way
darkness rose to claim the day.

Part II

Did mankind go retrograde?
Did darkness steal the light
from our age? Everyone
is filled with rage. Blinded,
we grope along looking for
answers on our phones
while driving to the store
to buy more ammo.

Living In The Land Of The Gun

What's it like living in the Land of the Gun?
Let me tell you right now: not much fun!

I mean, some days it feels like everyone's
got one. What the heck are they all protecting
themselves from -- each other? C'mon, man!

Don't we have police officers and sheriffs for
that? I scratch my head and wonder: Is this
really the Right Wing's version of freedom in
America? Because this isn't freedom. It's a

nightmare, not a dream: a culture where nuts
strut about with assault rifles and guns while
we citizens get slaughtered by the hundreds
(adults at concerts, children in schools) because
traitors in congress bow down to NRA fools.

This American culture with men spewing death
and toxic masculinity is so bad, so discouraging.
Gun nuts try and pass it off as normalcy. Really?
If this were true I'd have to give up on humanity.

It's hard to stay positive and not let the politicians
make me believe in their sick vision of protecting
the second amendment at all costs, even if that
means I have to die for it and you do, too. Look.

Christians don't own guns. Neither do they run
around killing shit. Did Jesus have one? No.
Now do me a favor: don't tell me I need one.

I am a child of God, an angel who temporarily
set his wings aside to experience life on earth
with all its pain and sadness, its joy and mirth.

I came from love and will return to love. While
here I try my best to be a healthy cell in the body
of humanity. I believe that's what God wants of me.

I don't know what else to tell you except that
it would come as no surprise to me at all if one
day I got shot by a nut with a gun simply because
I had the great misfortune to be born American.

It's like that, you see, in The Land of the Gun where
we walking dead keep a gallows sense of humor
and grim perspectives on our mortality because our
so-called leaders made a mockery of public safety
along with every word our Founding Fathers wrote.

In fact, our House of Representatives is a joke that
turns children into targets to be filled with bullet holes.

Oh, the tears in the eyes of the twenty Newton children
who knew they were going to die as they stared terrified
at Adam Lanza's assault rifle! They cried so hard, held

out their little arms for mommy and daddy as the bullets
tore them in two and cut them in half, shattered their skulls
and splattered their guts and brain matter on the walls.

Twenty lumps of dead flesh, blood running on the floor
and the monsters in the U. S. Senate did nothing at all.

Sorry kids. You gotta go. From Columbine to Parkland,
Maine to New Mexico. You all simply have to go. Why?
I already told you so! It's the sacred second amendment.
How many times do I have to tell you how precious it is?

So now you know the feeling we who live in The Land of
the Gun have about being sacrificed to the real terrorist:
an angry white American male with an assault rifle. Life
means nothing here. Seriously, it's just so much fun trying
to stay alive in America. Aren't you glad you don't live here?

What Those Who Have Been Tortured Know

Some people enjoy hurting others
and watching them suffer. Pleas fall
on deaf ears. You're on your own.

Why you were detained is a lie. Pain
is a place beyond words and begging
won't help. You will never be the same.

Fair had nothing to do with it. Justice?
Doesn't exist. Man's inhumanity to man
supersedes his tendency for kindness.
His capacity for cruelty is boundless.

Suffering drinks his fill at the trough
while mercy begs for water. You can
survive. You are stronger than you think.
What happened is incomprehensible.

Wax And Wicks

Oh my friends! The flame of knowledge burns low and dim
in this age of the internet and disinformation so we're going
to need more wax and wicks to light the way else the flame
burn out, surrendering to darkness. Mercury used to fly around.

Hermes followed close behind. People expanded their minds.
Knowledge was prized by all but then was slain by troglodytes
and simians. What the hell. Even Adam and Eve had their fall.

Oh flame of knowledge! Don't burn out. Lest we never know
the mysteries of the ages – Aratus, the Pleiades, Eratosthenes
Ptolemy and the riddle of the sphinx. No Descartes. No Spinoza.
No Leibnitz nor Hume. No Buddha. Confucius. Machu Picchu.
No pyramids or stars. No dreaming of Neptune, Jupiter or Mars.

Just oligarchs and billion-dollar yachts. Pathocracy and greed.
Corrupt elites with legions of homeless begging on the streets.

Man was once Icarus but twasn't the sun's rays melted his wings:
ignorance did the thing. More wax, then, for hapless Icarus and
the rest of us. Wax to hold the wicks upright and wicks to burn
the flame so bright. Kilos of wax and meters of wicks for this
age of darkness in which mothers and children get blown up
on bridges in Kiev. Wax, then; and wicks, to get us beyond this.

They're Killing All The Poets

They're killing all the poets. So sweetheart, I must go.
Franco's men took Lorca* and shot him in the snow.
Lorca was a gentle soul who wrote of love and freedom.
I do, too. Now my life's in danger and it's time to flee.

We thought a new age was dawning and glowing in
the east, and that man evolved and found a way to
bury hatred deep. But then he reverted back to beast.

So they arrested the professors and blamed the Jews.
They locked up the protesters and shut down the news.
No more voting booths. Secret police prowl the streets.
There's only state TV broadcasting lies and hypocrisy.
and in Katyn Forest,** pistol shots ringing off the trees.

Stalin got it early on when Mandelstam*** insulted him in
a poem. Now his bones lie with those of other poets in a
mass Siberian grave. It's never been different, no matter
the day or age. Dictators and tyrants silence dissent.

They fear many things indeed, especially poets with pens
who raise discontents in the hearts of men. Even in Algeria
as recently as 1993, poets Tahar Djaout and Youssef Sebti****
were murdered in the name of Islamic zealotry.

Poets sing an honest song before a righteous God, a simple act
that more often than not puts them in front of a firing squad.
Darkness ever tries to silence the truth and steal light from day.
Poets push back too much. And that is why they must be slayed.

* Spanish poet, 1898-1936. Executed during the Spanish Civil War.
** Site of 1940 mass execution of 22,000 Polish intellectuals by Russians.
*** Russian poet, 1891-1938.
**** Two of many Algerian artists murdered by the Islamic Salvation Front
in a wave of terror that year.

I Join The Gods Among The Stars

Ol' Prometheus. He really pissed the gods off
when he brought fire to man, a sin for which
he could not be forgiven. So Zeus chained him
to a rock and sent an eagle each day to eat his liver.

And talk about being done wrong: Andromeda
was blameless but also tied to a rock for sacrifice
to a sea dragon ravaging the coast in rage at
her mother, Queen Cassiopeia, who dared say
she was more beautiful than even the sea nymphs.

Then they of course demanded punishment for
for such sacrilege and audacity from the queen
who said *Take my daughter in place of me*.

Tantalus, son of Zeus, fared just as worse with his
curse, bound for all eternity was he to reach for fruit
on a tree that withdrew its branches each time
he touched it, and standing in water he could not
bend over to drink. Poor Tantalus, forever thirsty and
hungry because he stole ambrosia from the gods.

Sisyphus of course was forced to push a boulder up
a hill only to have it roll back again once he got it to
the top. He was such an excellent thief he cheated
death twice, which is why he had to pay that price.

Then there's me. I'm no god, but apparently I've
offended them since I, too, have a punishment.
I am chained to a rock -- the rock of poetry.

For I am odd and struck with verse. And then,
alas, I am also cursed to work without reward.
So each day an eagle and a dragon show up
to feast on me while I toil endlessly with words.

Fortune lights on few, indeed. That's the way
it seems to me. For I, too, have planted crops
and only come up with weeds. What, then,
shall be my stars? Something fiery like Antares?

Because while on Earth I burned so hot, pounding
words till their sparks shot off. I'll go to Mars, then.
Vulcan, too. They'll be my crew. Mars is red while
Vulcan's master of the forge. Once up there, I'll slam

my words against his mighty anvil while helping him
shape horseshoes for the gods in the stars. I'm sure
they'll put me in a dim-lit part of the sky no other stars
ever come by since that's the way it also was in life.

Wonder what they'll call me? Craigus Cadmus, perhaps?
Maybe William Wordsmith. No matter. I leave this Earth
this vale of tears, to join the gods among the stars.

I'm no damsel in distress and you can have Prometheus
Andromeda and Tantalus, too, as far as I'm concerned.
My original sin was words: I played with them and got burned.

About the Author

Literary omnivore. English M.A. Poet. Screenwriter. Short stories. Dreamer. Coffee connoisseur. Vegetarian. Peace advocate. Astronomer. Astrologer. Sun, Ascendant, Venus, Pluto and Mercury in Leo. Animal lover. Striving spirit, raging angel. Grandfather. 12-year Air Force veteran. Teacher. Editor. Insomniac. 100 mph guy in 50 mph world.

Editor, 6940th Security Wing newspaper, Goodfellow AFB, San Angelo, Texas.

Staff Writer, Airman Magazine, Kelly AFB, San Antonio, Texas.

Editor, Air Combat Command News Service, Langley AFB, Va.

City Hall Reporter, The Longview (Texas) News-Journal.

Writing Instructor, English and Business departments, University of Nebraska at Omaha and Metropolitan Community College.

www.ingramcontent.com/pod-product-compliance
Lightning Source LLC
Chambersburg PA
CBHW031311060726
47590CB00003B/1159